Betty Crocker

KIDS COOK!

Houghton Mifflin Harcourt
Boston New York

Copyright ©2007 by General Mills, Minneapolis, MN. All rights reserved.

Published by Houghton Mifflin Harcourt Publishing Company

For information about permission to reproduce selections from this book, please write Permissions, Houghton Mifflin Harcourt Publishing Company 215 Park Avenue South NY NY 10003.

www.hmhco.com

Library of Congress Cataloging-in-Publication Data:

Crocker, Betty.
  Betty Crocker kids cook!—2nd ed. / Betty Crocker.
    p. cm.
  Includes index.
  ISBN: 978-0-471-75309-4 (cloth)
    1. Cookery—Juvenile literature. I. Title.
  TX652.5.C688 2007
  641.5'622—dc22
                          2006022831

Manufactured in China

Toppan Leefung Packaging & Printing (Dongguan) Co., Ltd.

Jin Ju Guan Li Qu, Da Ling Shan Town, Dongguan, PRC

October 2009

TOP 10 9

4500464186

Cover illustration: Stephen Gilpin

General Mills

Publisher, Books and Magazines: Sheila Burke

Manager, Cookbook Publishing: Lois Tlusty

Editor: Heidi Losleben

Recipe Development and Testing: Betty Crocker Kitchens

Photography: General Mills Photography Studios and Image Library

Photographer: Mike Parker

Food Stylists: Carmen Bonilla and Nancy Johnson

Publisher: Natalie Chapman

Executive Editor: Anne Ficklen

Editor: Kristi Hart

Editorial Assistant: Charleen Barila

Production Manager: Leslie Anglin

Cover Design: Paul DiNovo

Illustrator: Stephen Gilpin

Art Director: Tai Blanche

Interior Design and Layout: Holly Wittenberg

Photography Art Direction: Paul DiNovo

Manufacturing Manager: Kevin Watt

Merry Christmas Joe !

Love,
Aunt Jane & Uncle Nels

TESTED & APPROVED — Betty Crocker® KITCHENS

The **Betty Crocker Kitchens** seal guarantees success in your kitchen. Every recipe has been tested in America's Most Trusted Kitchens™ to meet our high standards of reliability, easy preparation and great taste.

FIND MORE GREAT IDEAS AT
BettyCrocker.com

2014

Hey Kids!

Like to cook or want to learn? Then you've come to the right place. This cookbook is chock full of great-tasting, fun foods to make. Whatever you like to eat—breakfast, lunch, snacks, dinner or desserts—**Kids Cook!** has a way to manage your munchies. From Gooey Caramel Rolls, Chicken Lickin' Quesadillas and Purple Cow Shakes, to Trees with Cheese, Worth-Braggin'-About Burgers and Indoor S'mores. Is your mouth watering yet?

If you think watching cooking shows and chefs on TV is fun, wait until you start mixing up stuff in the kitchen yourself. Learning to cook is way more exciting when you get to eat the results (sometimes, even the mistakes taste good!). Before you know it, you'll be serving shakes to your friends and making muffins for Mother's Day.

The recipes are a cinch to make and every single one has a picture so you know what the food will look like when it's done. In the front of the book, you'll find some important safety tips (be sure to read 'em!), and a dictionary of useful cooking words. You'll also find ways to eat healthy and keep your body in tip-top shape.

Keep a Lookout For... You'll find the oven mitt at the beginning of some of the steps in the recipes. It means you might want to ask an adult to help you because you are using a sharp knife or handling something hot.

Look for the Chef's Choice tucked in the ingredients. Select your favorite of the three ingredients listed and make the recipe the way you like it best.

Follow the flower and check out the **How to...** pop-up for helpful cooking tips.

So come on, what are you waiting for? Roll up your sleeves and let's get cooking!

Have fun!
Betty Crocker

Table of

Contents

Kitchen ABCs

Play It Safe

Keep It Clean

- Wash your hands with warm, soapy water. Make sure to dry them really well so they're not slippery.

- Wear an apron or an old shirt so you don't get your clothes dirty. If your shirt has long sleeves, roll them up. If your hair is long, tie it back.

- Keep a roll of paper towels or a damp dishcloth nearby so you can wipe up any spills.

Stay Sharp

- If a recipe tells you to use something sharp, like a knife, a vegetable peeler or a can opener, ask an adult for help.

- When you use a knife to chop stuff, put the food on a cutting board—not on the kitchen counter.

- When you use a knife, make sure that the sharp edge of the knife is turned away from you.

Power Play

- Whenever you need to put in or take out the beaters of an electric mixer, first turn off the mixer and unplug it.

- Remember to turn the mixer off when you need to scrape the side of a bowl.

- Water and electricity don't mix. It's important to keep electrical appliances away from water to avoid getting a shock. Make sure your hands are dry, too.

Hot Pots (and Pans)!

- Turn the handles of saucepans and skillets into the center of the stove so you don't bump them and accidentally knock them off the stove.

- If you're stirring something on the stove, use a wooden spoon, not a metal one. A metal spoon can get hot, hot, hot!

- When you put pans in and out of the oven, you may want to ask an adult for help. Always use thick, dry pot holders.

Do the Math

3 teaspoons = 1 tablespoon

4 tablespoons = 1/4 cup

8 tablespoons = 1/2 cup

16 tablespoon = 1 cup

2 cups = 1 pint

4 cups = 1 quart

2 quarts = 1/2 gallon

1/2 cup butter = 1 stick of butter

Talk the Talk

Here are some good words to know when you cook or bake. If you have questions about what a word means, ask an adult for help.

BAKE: Cook food uncovered in the oven.

BEAT: Make a mixture smooth by stirring fast with a fork, wire whisk, eggbeater or electric mixer.

BOIL: Cook a liquid in a saucepan on top of the stove until big bubbles keep rising and breaking on the surface.

BROWN: Cook food until it looks brown on the outside.

CHOP: Cut food into small pieces on a cutting board, using a sharp knife. Don't worry if the pieces aren't the same shape, but they should be about the same size.

COOK: Make food for eating by heating it on top of the stove.

COOL: Put food on the counter (usually on a wire cooling rack) until it is no longer warm when you touch it. This is especially important if you will be frosting or decorating a cake or a batch of cookies. If you don't wait until the cake or cookies are completely cool, the frosting may start to melt.

COVER: Put a lid or a sheet of foil, waxed paper or plastic wrap over food. When you cook food on the stove, use a lid. When you put food in the oven, use foil. When you put food on the counter, in the refrigerator or in the freezer, use plastic wrap or foil. When you cook food in the microwave, use microwavable waxed paper or plastic wrap.

DRAIN: Pour off liquid or let it run out through the holes in a strainer or colander (see page 00). You do this to drain the water after you cook pasta or to drain the fat after you cook ground beef.

FREEZE: Put food in the freezer until it is frozen and hard as a rock.

GRATE: Rub an ingredient against the smallest holes on a grater to cut it into very small pieces.

GREASE: Spread the bottom and sides of a pan with shortening, butter or margarine, using a pastry brush or paper towel. You also can use cooking spray, which comes in a can. By greasing a pan, you will keep food from sticking to it.

KNEAD: Make dough smooth and stretchy by curving your fingers around and folding the dough toward you, then pushing it away with the heels of your hands, using a quick rocking motion.

MELT: Put a solid ingredient, such as chocolate or butter, in a saucepan and turn it into a liquid by heating it on the stove. You also can put the ingredient in a microwavable bowl and heat it in the microwave oven until melted.

MIX: Stir ingredients with a spoon, fork, eggbeater, wire whisk or electric mixer until smooth or almost smooth.

PEEL: Cut off the outer skin of fruits and vegetables, using a vegetable peeler or small sharp knife. You can peel some fruit, such as oranges and bananas, with your fingers.

REFRIGERATE: Put food in the refrigerator until it is cold.

SHRED: Rub an ingredient against the big holes on a grater to cut it into long, skinny pieces.

SLICE: Starting at one end, cut food into flat pieces on a cutting board, using a sharp knife. The pieces should all be about the same thickness.

TOSS: Mix ingredients by lifting them with a spoon or fork and letting them drop back into a bowl or pan. You do this when you make a "tossed salad."

You Are What You Eat

Every day you make choices about what to eat. Sometimes grown-ups make your choices for you. Other times, you're on your own. Some foods, like bananas, whole wheat bread and milk, give you energy, make you strong and keep your whole body running smoothly. Other foods, like candy, cookies and soda—even though they taste yummy—aren't as good for you.

To help you make smart choices, the U.S. Department of Agriculture (USDA) created a pyramid. The colored stripes represent the five food groups as well as oils and fats. The wider the stripe, the more food from that group you should eat. (Want to learn more about the Food Guide Pyramid? Go to mypyramid.gov.)

Calories are also something you should keep in mind when you eat. Calories keep you going, kind of like how gas keeps a car moving. You burn off calories when you exercise. If you eat more calories than you get rid of, you gain weight. The guy climbing up the Pyramid is a reminder that exercise is also important to staying healthy. So get outside and have fun!

Grains

What They Are: Bread, oatmeal, rice, pasta and cereal

What They Do for You: Provide carbohydrates, which give you lots of energy for running, jumping and playing

How Much You Need Every Day:

Boys ages 9 to 13 need 6 ounces.

Girls ages 9 to 13 need 5 ounces.

(One ounce is about 1 slice of bread or 1/2 cup oatmeal or 1 cup of cold cereal.)

Vegetables

What They Are: Corn, carrots, green beans, peas, tomatoes and, yes, broccoli

What They Do for You: Give you lots of vitamins and minerals, which help you see well and have shiny hair and clear skin

How Much You Need Every Day:

Boys ages 9 to 13 need 2 1/2 cups.

Girls ages 9 to 13 need 2 cups.

Fruits

What They Are: Strawberries, apples, raisins, grapes, bananas, pears, cherries, raspberries and blueberries

What They Do for You: Give you lots of vitamins and minerals, which help your heart and muscles work well and carry oxygen to all the cells in your body

How Much You Need Every Day: Boys and girls ages 9 to 13 need 1 1/2 cups.

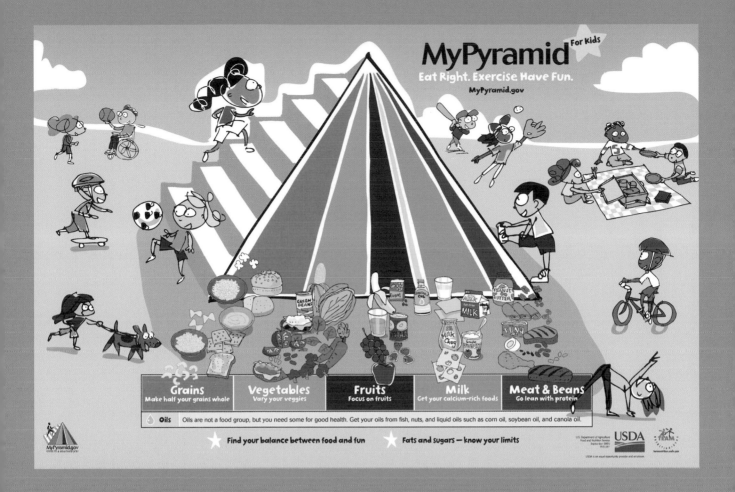

Milk
(and Other Calcium-Rich Foods)

What They Are: Milk, of course, plus yogurt and cheese

What They Do for You: Build strong teeth and bones

How Much You Need Every Day: Boys and girls ages 9 to 13 need 3 cups.

Meat & Beans

What They Are: Chicken, beef, fish, eggs, beans and peanuts

What They Do for You: Provide protein and iron to make your muscles grow and keep you strong

How Much You Need Every Day: Boys and girls ages 9 to 13 need 5 ounces. (One ounce is about 1 egg, 1 tablespoon of peanut butter or 1/4 cup of cooked dry beans.)

Oils & Fats

What They Are: Cooking oil, butter and salad dressing are three examples

What They Do for You: Keep your brain working and carry vitamins around in your body

How Much You Need Every Day: Boys and girls ages 9 to 13 need about 5 teaspoons.

Bring On Breakfast!

Berry-licious

Prep 10 minutes
Cook 8 minutes
Makes 9 pancakes (4 inch)

Ingredients

1 egg

1 cup all-purpose flour or whole wheat flour

3/4 cup milk

1 tablespoon granulated sugar or packed brown sugar

2 tablespoons vegetable oil

3 teaspoons baking powder

1/4 teaspoon salt

3 Pancakes: Calories 330 (Calories from Fat 120); Total Fat 13g (Saturated Fat 2.5g; Trans Fat 0g); Cholesterol 75mg; Sodium 730mg; Total Carbohydrate 44g (Dietary Fiber 2g; Sugars 10g); Protein 9g **% Daily Value:** Vitamin A 4%; Vitamin C 2%; Calcium 35%; Iron 15% **Exchanges:** 3 Starch, 2 Fat **Carbohydrate Choices:** 3

Pancakes

1/2 cup fresh or frozen
(thawed and well drained) blueberries

or 1/2 cup fresh or frozen (thawed
and well drained) raspberries

or 1/2 cup fresh or frozen (thawed
and well drained) blackberries

Cooking spray

Butter or margarine, if you like

Maple-flavored syrup, if you like

Blueberries and raspberries,
if you like

1

Crack the **EGG** on side of the bowl, letting egg slip into bowl. Beat with the fork until egg looks foamy. Add the **FLOUR**, **MILK**, **GRANULATED SUGAR**, **VEGETABLE OIL**, **BAKING POWDER** and **SALT**. Beat with the fork until mixture is smooth. (For thinner pancakes, stir in 1 to 2 tablespoons milk.) Stir the **BLUEBERRIES** (or **RASPBERRIES** or **BLACKBERRIES**) into the batter.

2

Spray the unheated griddle or electric skillet with the **COOKING SPRAY**. Heat griddle over medium heat, or heat electric skillet to 375°F. (To test griddle or skillet, sprinkle with just a few drops of water. If bubbles jump around, heat is just right.)

3

For each pancake, pour about 1/4 cup of batter from the measuring cup onto hot griddle or skillet. Cook for about 2 minutes or until pancakes are puffy and dry around the edges. Turn the pancakes over, using the pancake turner. Cook for about 2 minutes or until bottoms of pancakes are golden brown.

4

Serve pancakes with butter, maple-flavored syrup and berries, if you like.

Utensils

Medium mixing bowl
Fork
Dry-ingredient measuring cups
Liquid-ingredient measuring cup
Measuring spoons
Griddle or electric skillet
Pancake turner
Table knife

Fabulous French Toast Stix

Ingredients

4 slices bread
3 eggs
1/4 cup milk
2 cups cornflakes cereal

1 tablespoon butter or margarine
Maple-flavored syrup or powdered sugar, if you like

Prep 20 minutes
Cook 8 minutes
Makes 12 "stix"

Utensils

Cutting board
Serrated knife
Rectangular glass baking dish
(13 × 9 inch; 3 quart)
Medium mixing bowl
Liquid-ingredient measuring cup

Fork
Pancake turner
Dry-ingredient measuring cups
Plastic bag with zipper top
Rolling pin
Shallow dish or pie plate
Table knife
Extra-large skillet (12 inch)

1 Cut each slice of **BREAD** into 3 strips on the cutting board, using the serrated knife. Put bread strips in the baking dish.

2 Crack the **EGGS** on side of the bowl, letting eggs slip into bowl. Add the **MILK** to eggs. Beat with the fork until eggs look foamy. Pour over bread in baking dish. Turn bread strips over, using the pancake turner, to coat other side.

3 Put the **CEREAL** in the plastic bag. Seal bag closed. Use the rolling pin to crush cereal. Dump crushed cereal into the shallow dish or pie plate.

4 Put the **BUTTER** in the skillet. Heat over medium heat until butter is melted (you can tilt the skillet so inside of skillet will be coated with butter).

5 Take the bread strips out of egg mixture, using pancake turner, and put them on the crushed cereal. Turn bread strips over, using pancake turner, to coat other sides.

6 Put the cereal-coated bread strips into the hot skillet. Cook for about 4 minutes or until bottoms of bread strips are golden brown (you can lift an edge with the pancake turner and peek). Turn bread strips over. Cook on other sides for about 4 minutes or until bottoms are golden brown.

7 Serve the "stix" with the **SYRUP** or sprinkle with **POWDERED SUGAR**, if you like.

3 "stix": Calories 210 (Calories from Fat 70); Total Fat 8g (Saturated Fat 3.5g; Trans Fat 0g); Cholesterol 170mg; Sodium 340mg; Total Carbohydrate 26g (Dietary Fiber 1g; Sugars 3g); Protein 8g   % Daily Value: Vitamin A 10%; Vitamin C 2%; Calcium 8%; Iron 30%   Exchanges: 1 1/2 Starch, 1/2 Medium-Fat Meat, 1 Fat   Carbohydrate Choices: 2

Oooh-La-La Omelet

Prep 5 minutes
Cook 5 minutes
Makes 1 serving

Ingredients

2 eggs

2 teaspoons butter or margarine

 Chef's Choice

1/4 cup shredded Cheddar cheese
or 1/4 cup diced cooked ham
or 1/4 cup chopped tomato

Salt and pepper, if you like

Utensils

Small mixing bowl
Fork
Table knife
Medium skillet (8 inch)
Pancake turner
Dry-ingredient measuring cups

1 Crack the **EGGS** on side of the bowl, letting eggs slip into bowl. Beat with the fork until eggs look foamy.

2 Put the **BUTTER** in the skillet. Heat over medium heat until butter is melted (you can tilt the skillet so inside of skillet will be coated with butter).

3 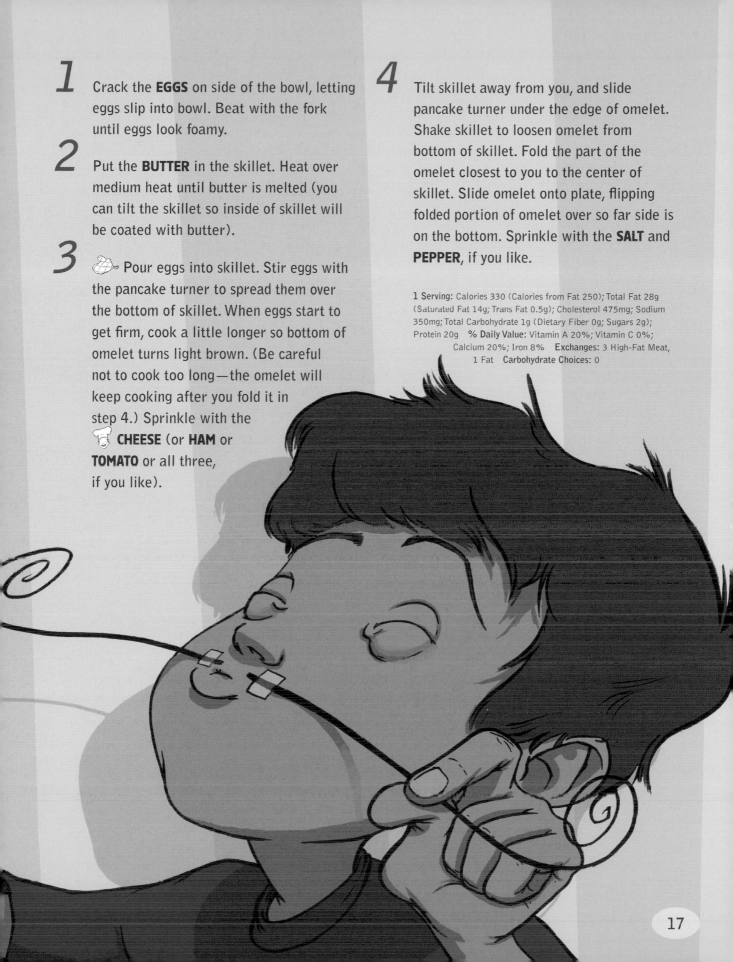 Pour eggs into skillet. Stir eggs with the pancake turner to spread them over the bottom of skillet. When eggs start to get firm, cook a little longer so bottom of omelet turns light brown. (Be careful not to cook too long—the omelet will keep cooking after you fold it in step 4.) Sprinkle with the **CHEESE** (or **HAM** or **TOMATO** or all three, if you like).

4 Tilt skillet away from you, and slide pancake turner under the edge of omelet. Shake skillet to loosen omelet from bottom of skillet. Fold the part of the omelet closest to you to the center of skillet. Slide omelet onto plate, flipping folded portion of omelet over so far side is on the bottom. Sprinkle with the **SALT** and **PEPPER**, if you like.

1 Serving: Calories 330 (Calories from Fat 250); Total Fat 28g (Saturated Fat 14g; Trans Fat 0.5g); Cholesterol 475mg; Sodium 350mg; Total Carbohydrate 1g (Dietary Fiber 0g; Sugars 2g); Protein 20g   % Daily Value: Vitamin A 20%; Vitamin C 0%; Calcium 20%; Iron 8%   Exchanges: 3 High-Fat Meat, 1 Fat   Carbohydrate Choices: 0

Scrambled-Up Eggs

Prep 5 minutes
Cook 6 minutes
Makes 4 servings

Utensils

Medium mixing bowl
Liquid-ingredient measuring cup
Measuring spoons
Fork or wire whisk
Table knife
Large skillet (10 inch)
Pancake turner

Ingredients

6 eggs
1/3 cup water, milk
or half-and-half
1/4 teaspoon salt
1/8 teaspoon pepper, if you like
1 tablespoon butter
or margarine

1 Crack the **EGGS** on side of the bowl, letting eggs slip into bowl. Add the **WATER**, **SALT** and **PEPPER** (if you like) to eggs. Beat with the fork until eggs look foamy.

2 Put the **BUTTER** in the skillet. Heat over medium heat just until butter begins to sizzle (you can tilt the skillet so inside of skillet will be coated with butter).

3 Pour the egg mixture into skillet and cook without stirring. When eggs in bottom of skillet start to get firm, stir eggs gently with the pancake turner. Cook for 3 to 4 minutes longer or until eggs are slightly firm but not runny.

1 Serving: Calories 140 (Calories from Fat 100); Total Fat 11g (Saturated Fat 4.5g; Trans Fat 0g); Cholesterol 325mg; Sodium 260mg; Total Carbohydrate 0g (Dietary Fiber 0g; Sugars 0g); Protein 9g   % Daily Value: Vitamin A 10%; Vitamin C 0%; Calcium 4%; Iron 4%   Exchanges: 1 1/2 Medium-Fat Meat, 1/2 Fat   Carbohydrate Choices: 0

Egg-cellent Breakfast Bake

Ingredients

Cooking spray

Chef's Choice

1 cup cooked crumbled sausage
or 1/2 cup bacon-flavor bits or chips
or 1 cup diced cooked ham (6 ounces)

2 boxes (5.2 ounces each) hash brown potatoes mix

1 tablespoon dried chopped onion

1 bag (8 ounces) shredded Cheddar cheese (2 cups)

4 eggs

3 cups milk

1 cup Original Bisquick® or
Bisquick Heart Smart™ mix

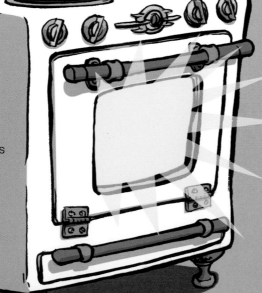

Prep 12 minutes
Refrigerate 4 hours
Bake 35 minutes
Cool 10 minutes
Makes 12 servings

Utensils

Rectangular glass baking dish
(13 × 9 inch; 3 quart)
Dry-ingredient measuring cups
Measuring spoons
Wooden spoon
Medium mixing bowl
Liquid-ingredient measuring cup
Fork
Plastic wrap
Pot holders
Sharp knife

1 Spray bottom and sides of the baking dish with the **COOKING SPRAY**. Put the **SAUSAGE** (or **BACON BITS** or **HAM**), **POTATOES**, **ONION** and half (1 cup) of the **CHEESE** in baking dish. Stir with the wooden spoon until mixed. Spread the mixture evenly in bottom of dish, using back of spoon.

2 Crack the **EGGS** on side of the bowl, letting eggs slip into bowl. Add the **MILK** and **BISQUICK MIX** to eggs. Beat with the fork until mixed. Pour the egg mixture into dish. Sprinkle with the rest of cheese. Cover dish

with the plastic wrap and put it in the refrigerator for at least 4 hours but no longer than 24 hours (the bread needs time to soak up the eggs).

3 Heat the oven to 375°F. Take plastic wrap off dish and bake for 30 to 35 minutes or until the breakfast bake is light golden brown around the edges and cheese is melted. Use the pot holders to take dish out of oven—it will be very hot and heavy. Cool for 10 minutes. Cut it into 6 rows by 6 rows, using the knife.

1 Serving: Calories 280 (Calories from Fat 110); Total Fat 12g (Saturated Fat 6g; Trans Fat 0g); Cholesterol 100mg; Sodium 490mg; Total Carbohydrate 30g (Dietary Fiber 2g; Sugars 5g); Protein 14g   % Daily Value: Vitamin A 8%; Vitamin C 0%; Calcium 20%; Iron 8%   Exchanges: 2 Starch, 1 High-Fat Meat, 1/2 Fat   Carbohydrate Choices: 2

Apple-a-Day Oatmeal

Ingredients

1/3 cup quick-cooking oats

3/4 cup apple juice or
apple cider

1 pouch (about 3/4 ounce)
chewy fruit snacks shapes
(any flavor)

Prep 5 minutes
Microwave 2 minutes 30 seconds
Cool 1 minute
Makes 1 serving

Utensils

Dry-ingredient measuring cups
Liquid-ingredient measuring cup
Large microwavable mug
Spoon
Pot holders

1 Put the **OATS** and **APPLE JUICE** in the mug. Stir with the spoon until mixed.

2 Microwave mug on High 1 minute. Use the pot holders to take mug out of microwave. Stir with spoon. Microwave 30 seconds to 1 minute 30 seconds longer or until oats and apple juice are thick when stirred. Use pot holders to take mug out of microwave.

3 Add the **FRUIT SNACKS** to oatmeal. Stir with spoon until mixed. Cool 1 minute before eating.

1 Serving: Calories 270 (Calories from Fat 15); Total Fat 2g (Saturated Fat 0g; Trans Fat 0g); Cholesterol 0mg; Sodium 50mg; Total Carbohydrate 58g (Dietary Fiber 3g; Sugars 28g); Protein 5g   **% Daily Value:** Vitamin A 0%; Vitamin C 10%; Calcium 2%; Iron 10%   **Exchanges:** 2 Starch, 2 Other Carbohydrate   **Carbohydrate Choices:** 4

Mouthwatering Cinnamon Muffins

Prep 25 minutes
Bake 25 minutes
Microwave 1 minute
Cool 5 minutes
Makes 12 muffins

Ingredients

Cooking spray
1/2 cup sugar
1/2 cup milk
1/3 cup vegetable oil
1 egg
1 1/2 cups all-purpose flour
1 1/2 teaspoons baking powder
1/2 teaspoon salt

1/4 teaspoon ground nutmeg
1/2 cup sugar
1 teaspoon ground cinnamon
1/2 cup (1 stick) butter or margarine

Utensils

Muffin pan with 12 regular-size cups
Dry-ingredient measuring cups
Liquid-ingredient measuring cup
Medium mixing bowl
2 wooden spoons
Fork
Measuring spoons

Toothpick
Small mixing bowl
Shallow microwavable bowl and microwavable waxed paper
Pot holders
Wire cooling rack

1 Heat the oven to 350°F. Spray just the bottoms of each cup in the muffin pan with the **COOKING SPRAY**. Save for later (you will need this in step 3).

2 Put the first 1/2 cup **SUGAR**, the **MILK** and **VEGETABLE OIL** in the medium bowl. Stir with one of the wooden spoons until mixed. Crack the **EGG** on side of bowl, letting it slip into bowl. Beat with the fork until mixed.

3 Add the **FLOUR**, **BAKING POWDER**, **SALT** and **NUTMEG** to sugar mixture. Stir just until flour is wet (the batter should still be a little lumpy; you don't want it to be smooth). Spoon batter into sprayed muffin cups until cups are about 2/3 full.

4 Bake for 20 to 25 minutes or until the muffins are until golden brown and the toothpick poked in center of muffin comes out clean.

5 While muffins are baking, mix the second 1/2 cup **SUGAR** and the **CINNAMON** in the small bowl. Save for later (you will need this in step 8).

6 Put the **BUTTER** in the microwavable bowl. Cover bowl with microwavable waxed paper. Microwave on High for 30 to 45 seconds or until butter is melted. Cool for 5 minutes.

7 Use the pot holders to take muffin pan out of oven. Carefully tip pan on its side to take muffins out of cups. Put muffins on the wire cooling rack. Cool for 5 minutes.

8 First roll muffins in the melted butter. Then roll them in the sugar-cinnamon mixture so they are coated. Serve warm.

1 Muffin: Calories 260 (Calories from Fat 140); Total Fat 15g (Saturated Fat 6g; Trans Fat 0g); Cholesterol 40mg; Sodium 220mg; Total Carbohydrate 29g (Dietary Fiber 0g; Sugars 17g); Protein 3g % Daily Value: Vitamin A 6%; Vitamin C 0%; Calcium 6%; Iron 6% Exchanges: 1 Starch, 1 Other Carbohydrate, 3 Fat Carbohydrate Choices: 2

Prep 20 minutes
Cook 1 minute
Bake 1 hour 15 minutes
Cool 10 minutes
Makes 1 loaf (16 slices)

Banana-o-Rama Bread

Ingredients

Cooking spray
3 medium bananas
1/2 cup (1 stick) butter or margarine
2 eggs
1 1/2 cups sugar
1/2 cup buttermilk
1 teaspoon vanilla
2 1/2 cups all-purpose flour
1 teaspoon baking soda
1 teaspoon salt

Utensils

Loaf pan (9 × 5 inch)
Large mixing bowl
Potato masher or fork
Small saucepan (1 quart) or microwavable
bowl and microwavable waxed paper
Wooden spoon
Dry-ingredient measuring cups
Liquid-ingredient measuring cup
Measuring spoons
Toothpick
Pot holders
Table knife
Wire cooling rack

1 Heat the oven to 350°F. Spray just the bottom of the pan with the **COOKING SPRAY**.
Save for later (you will need this in step 5).

2 Peel the **BANANAS**. Put bananas in the bowl. Mash bananas with the potato
masher or fork until almost smooth.

3 Put the **BUTTER** in the saucepan. Heat over low heat for about 1 minute, stirring a few times with the wooden spoon, until butter is melted. Take saucepan off hot burner. (Or put butter in the microwavable bowl. Cover bowl with the microwavable waxed paper. Microwave butter on High for 30 to 45 seconds or until it is melted.) Cool for 5 minutes.

4 Crack the **EGGS** on side of bowl with bananas in it, letting eggs slip into bowl. Add melted butter, the **SUGAR**, **BUTTERMILK** and **VANILLA**. Stir with spoon until mixed.

5 Add the **FLOUR**, **BAKING SODA** and **SALT** to banana mixture. Stir just until flour is wet. Pour the batter into the sprayed pan.

✳ How to...

...Take the Bread Out of the Pan: Loosen the sides of bread from pan, using the knife. Carefully tip pan on its side and tap gently so the bread comes out.

6 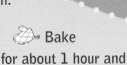 Bake for about 1 hour and 15 minutes or until the toothpick poked in center of bread comes out clean. Use the pot holders to take pan out of oven. Cool bread in pan for 5 minutes.

7 Take bread out of pan. ✳ Put bread on the wire cooling rack and let it sit until it is no longer warm when you touch it.

1 Slice: Calories 230 (Calories from Fat 60); Total Fat 7g (Saturated Fat 4g; Trans Fat 0g); Cholesterol 40mg; Sodium 280mg; Total Carbohydrate 39g (Dietary Fiber 1g; Sugars 22g); Protein 3g **% Daily Value:** Vitamin A 4%; Vitamin C 0%; Calcium 2%; Iron 6% **Exchanges:** 1 Starch, 1 1/2 Other Carbohydrate, 1 1/2 Fat **Carbohydrate Choices:** 2 1/2

Gooey Caramel Rolls

Prep 20 minutes
Bake 25 minutes
Cool 2 minutes
Makes 6 rolls

Ingredients

1/2 cup packed dark brown sugar
1/3 cup whipping cream
1/4 cup chopped pecans
2 tablespoons granulated sugar
1 teaspoon ground cinnamon
1 can (11 ounces) refrigerated original breadsticks

Utensils

Dry-ingredient measuring cups
Liquid-ingredient measuring cup
Round cake pan (8 inch)
Wooden spoon
Measuring spoons
Small mixing bowl
Sharp knife
Pot holders
Large heatproof plate

1 Heat the oven to 350°F. Put the **BROWN SUGAR** and **WHIPPING CREAM** in the cake pan. Stir with the wooden spoon until mixed. Sprinkle with the **PECANS**. Save for later (you will need this in step 4).

2 Put the **GRANULATED SUGAR** and **CINNAMON** in the bowl. Stir with spoon until mixed.

3 Open the can of **BREADSTICKS** and take out the dough. Unroll dough, but do not separate it into breadsticks. Sprinkle the cinnamon-sugar mixture over dough. Roll up dough, starting at one of the short sides.

4 Separate the dough at the cut marks into spiral slices, using the knife. Put the dough slices on top of the sauce in pan.

5 Bake for **25** minutes or until the rolls are golden brown. Use the pot holders to take pan out of oven. Cool for 1 minute. Put the plate, upside down, over pan. With pot holders, pick up plate and pan, then turn both over. Leave pan over rolls for 1 minute so sauce will drizzle over rolls. Take pan off rolls.

1 Roll: Calories 310 (Calories from Fat 100); Total Fat 11g (Saturated Fat 4g; Trans Fat 1g); Cholesterol 20mg; Sodium 380mg; Total Carbohydrate 48g (Dietary Fiber 1g; Sugars 25g); Protein 5g   % Daily Value: Vitamin A 4%; Vitamin C 0%; Calcium 4%; Iron 10%   Exchanges: 1 1/2 Starch, 1 1/2 Other Carbohydrate, 2 Fat   Carbohydrate Choices: 3

Fruity

Ingredients

2 medium bananas
2 cups vanilla fat-free yogurt

 Chef's Choice

1 cup frozen strawberries
or 1 cup frozen blueberries
or 1 cup frozen raspberries

1 cup orange juice

Utensils

Cutting board
Table knife
Blender with lid
Liquid-ingredient measuring cup
Dry-ingredient measuring cups
4 drinking glasses

Prep 10 minutes
Makes 4 servings

1 Peel the **BANANAS**. Cut each banana into chunks on the cutting board, using the knife. Put the banana chunks in the blender.

2 Add the **YOGURT**, **STRAWBERRIES** (or **BLUEBERRIES** or **RASPBERRIES**) and **ORANGE JUICE** to the bananas. Cover blender with lid, and blend on high speed about 30 seconds or until the mixture is smooth. Pour the smoothie into the glasses. Serve right away.

1 Serving: Calories 260 (Calories from Fat 0); Total Fat 0g (Saturated Fat 0g; Trans Fat 0g); Cholesterol 0mg; Sodium 65mg; Total Carbohydrate 57g (Dietary Fiber 5g; Sugars 46g); Protein 6g   **% Daily Value:** Vitamin A 2%; Vitamin C 90%; Calcium 20%; Iron 4%   **Exchanges:** 2 Fruit, 1 Other Carbohydrate, 1 Skim Milk   **Carbohydrate Choices:** 4

Smoothies

Let's Have Lunch

Join-the-Club Sandwiches

Prep 15 minutes
Makes 4 sandwiches

Ingredients

12 slices bread, toasted if you like
2 medium tomatoes
Mayonnaise or salad dressing
1/3 cup bacon flavor bits or chips
8 lettuce leaves
3/4 pound sliced cooked turkey

Utensils

Toaster, if you like
Paper towels
Cutting board
Sharp knife
Table knife
Dry-ingredient measuring cups
Measuring spoons
16 toothpicks

1 Sandwich: Calories 410 (Calories from Fat 130);
Total Fat 15g (Saturated Fat 2.5g; Trans Fat 0.5g);
Cholesterol 45mg; Sodium 1680mg; Total Carbohydrate 45g
(Dietary Fiber 3g; Sugars 8g); Protein 24g   % Daily
Value: Vitamin A 10%; Vitamin C 15%; Calcium 15%;
Iron 20%   Exchanges: 3 Starch, 2 Lean Meat,
1 1/2 Fat   Carbohydrate Choices: 3

1.  Toast the slices of **BREAD**, if you like. Wash the **TOMATOES** in cool water. Pat dry with the paper towels. Cut each tomato into 6 thin slices on the cutting board, using the sharp knife.

2. Spread the **MAYONNAISE** evenly on 1 side of each bread slice, using the table knife. Sprinkle about 1 teaspoon of the **BACON BITS** on top of each slice of bread.

3. Put 1 **LETTUCE LEAF** and 3 slices of tomato on each of 4 slices bread. Top each with another slice of bread, with the bacon bits on top. Put some **TURKEY** on top of the bacon bits. Put another lettuce leaf on top of the turkey. Top each with a third slice of bread, this time with the bacon bits side down. From bottom to top, your sandwich should be stacked like this: bread, mayonnaise, bacon bits, lettuce, 3 tomato slices, bread, mayonnaise, bacon bits, turkey, lettuce, bacon bits, mayonnaise, bread.

4. Cut each sandwich diagonally in half on the cutting board, with the sharp knife. Then cut these triangles in half again to make smaller triangles. Poke a toothpick in the center of each triangle to hold sandwich together. Before eating the sandwiches, be sure to remove the toothpicks!

Prep 15 minutes
Makes 6 sandwiches

Sub sandwiches

1 Sandwich: Calories 540 (Calories from Fat 260); Total Fat 29g (Saturated Fat 13g; Trans Fat 1g); Cholesterol 85mg; Sodium 1490mg; Total Carbohydrate 44g (Dietary Fiber 3g; Sugars 5g); Protein 26g   **% Daily Value:** Vitamin A 20%; Vitamin C 35%; Calcium 25%; Iron 20%   **Exchanges:** 2 1/2 Starch, 1 Vegetable, 2 1/2 Medium-Fat Meat, 3 Fat   **Carbohydrate Choices:** 3

Ingredients

1 loaf (1 pound) French bread
1/4 cup (1/2 stick) butter or margarine, softened
1 medium onion, if you like
2 medium tomatoes
1 medium green bell pepper
4 slices (1 ounce each) Swiss cheese
1/2 pound deli salami, sliced
2 cups shredded lettuce

Chef's Choice

1/2 pound fully cooked deli turkey, thinly sliced

or 1/2 pound fully cooked deli ham, thinly sliced

or 1/2 pound fully cooked deli chicken, thinly sliced

1 1/4 cup Italian dressing

1
 Cut the **BREAD** in half to make a top and a bottom on the cutting board, using the serrated knife. Spread the **BUTTER** evenly on the bottom half of bread, using the table knife.

2
If you use the **ONION**, peel off the outside layer of skin. Wash onion, **TOMATO** and **GREEN PEPPER** in cool water. Pat dry with the paper towels. Cut the onion, tomato and green pepper into thin slices on the cutting board, using the sharp knife. Remove the seeds and white stuff from inside the green pepper rings.

3
Layer the **CHEESE**, **SALAMI**, **LETTUCE**, tomato, onion, **TURKEY** (or **HAM** or **CHICKEN**) and green pepper on bottom half of bread.

4
Drizzle the **ITALIAN DRESSING** on the vegetables, cheese and meats. Put the top half of bread on the sandwich. Poke the wooden picks into sandwich, 1 for each serving, to hold it together. Cut sandwich into 6 pieces on cutting board, using sharp knife. Before eating, remove the wooden picks.

Utensils

Cutting board
Serrated knife
Table knife
Paper towels
Sharp knife
Dry-ingredient measuring cups
Liquid-ingredient measuring cup
6 long wooden picks or small skewers

Double-Decker

Ingredients

3 tablespoons butter or margarine, softened

8 slices bread

4 slices (3/4 ounce each) Cheddar cheese

4 slices (3/4 ounce each) Monterey Jack
or mozzarella cheese

Prep 10 minutes
Cook 8 minutes
Makes 4 sandwiches

Utensils

Table knife

Extra-large skillet (12 inch)

Pancake turner

Grilled Cheese Sandwiches

1 Spread the **BUTTER** evenly on 1 side of each **BREAD** slice, using the knife.

2 Put 4 slices of bread with buttered sides down in the skillet. Top each with 1 slice of **CHEDDAR CHEESE** and 1 slice of **MONTEREY JACK** cheese. Top with the other 4 slices of bread, buttered sides up.

3 Cook uncovered over medium heat for about 5 minutes or until the bottoms of the sandwiches are golden brown. Turn sandwiches over, using the pancake turner. Cook 2 to 3 minutes longer or until the bottoms are golden brown and cheese is melted.

1 Sandwich: Calories 370 (Calories from Fat 210); Total Fat 24g (Saturated Fat 14g; Trans Fat 1g); Cholesterol 65mg; Sodium 650mg; Total Carbohydrate 26g (Dietary Fiber 1g; Sugars 3g); Protein 14g   **% Daily Value:** Vitamin A 15%; Vitamin C 0%; Calcium 35%; Iron 10%   **Exchanges:** 1 1/2 Starch, 1 1/2 High-Fat Meat, 2 1/2 Fat Carbohydrate Choices: 2

Egg Salad Buns

Prep 15 minutes
Cook 3 minutes
Stand 20 minutes
Makes 12 buns

40

Ingredients

6 eggs

Cold water

1 medium stalk celery

3 tablespoons pickle relish

3 tablespoons mayonnaise
or salad dressing

12 mini hamburger buns, split

3/4 cup canned shoestring potatoes

Utensils

Medium saucepan
with lid (2 quart)

Kitchen timer

Medium mixing bowl

Table knife

Paper towels

Cutting board

Sharp knife

Dry-ingredient measuring cups

Measuring spoons

Wooden spoon

1 Put the **EGGS** in the saucepan. Add enough **COLD WATER** to saucepan until water covers eggs.

2 Heat the water and eggs to boiling over high heat. Take saucepan off hot burner. Cover saucepan with lid, and put on the counter and set kitchen timer for 20 minutes. After 20 minutes, run cold water into the saucepan to quickly cool eggs and keep them from cooking more.

3 Tap each egg lightly on the counter to crack the shell. Roll egg between your hands to loosen shell, then peel it off. (If shell is hard to peel, you can hold the egg under cold water while peeling.) Put the peeled eggs in the bowl. Chop the eggs into small pieces, using the table knife.

4 Wash the **CELERY** in cool water. Pat dry with the paper towels. Chop celery into small pieces on the cutting board, using the sharp knife (you need about 1/2 cup). Put the celery, **PICKLE RELISH** and **MAYONNAISE** in bowl with eggs. Stir until mixed, using the wooden spoon.

5 Split each **HAMBURGER BUN** in half to make a top and a bottom. Spoon egg salad mixture onto the bottoms of the buns. Sprinkle with the **SHOESTRING POTATOES**. Cover with the tops of buns.

3 Buns: Calories 450 (Calories from Fat 190); Total Fat 22g (Saturated Fat 5g; Trans Fat 0.5g); Cholesterol 320mg; Sodium 630mg; Total Carbohydrate 46g (Dietary Fiber 2g; Sugars 10g); Protein 17g   **% Daily Value:** Vitamin A 10%; Vitamin C 4%; Calcium 15%; Iron 20%   **Exchanges:** 3 Starch, 1 Medium-Fat Meat, 3 Fat   **Carbohydrate Choices:** 3

Burrito

Ingredients

8 slices bacon
1 large tomato
2 cups shredded lettuce
1 1/2 cups shredded Cheddar cheese (6 ounces)
1/3 cup mayonnaise or salad dressing
6 flour tortillas (8 to 10 inches across)

Utensils

Microwavable plate or rack
Microwavable paper towels
Pot holders
Cutting board
Sharp knife
Dry-ingredient measuring cups
Medium mixing bowl
Wooden spoon

Prep 10 minutes
Microwave 6 minutes
Makes 6 wraps

1 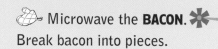 Microwave the **BACON**. ✳ Break bacon into pieces.

2 Wash the **TOMATO** in cool water. Pat dry with the paper towels. Chop tomato into small pieces on the cutting board, using the sharp knife.

1 Wrap: Calories 410 (Calories from Fat 240); Total Fat 27g (Saturated Fat 10g; Trans Fat 0.5g); Cholesterol 45mg; Sodium 700mg; Total Carbohydrate 26g (Dietary Fiber 2g; Sugars 2g); Protein 15g   **% Daily Value:** Vitamin A 15%; Vitamin C 8%; Calcium 20%; Iron 10%   **Exchanges:** 1 1/2 Starch, 1 1/2 High-Fat Meat, 3 Fat   **Carbohydrate Choices:** 2

BLT Wraps

3 Put the bacon, tomato, **LETTUCE**, **CHEDDAR CHEESE** and **MAYONNAISE** in the bowl. Toss together with the wooden spoon.

4 Spread the BLT mixture evenly on each of the **TORTILLAS**. Fold up the bottom third of each tortilla, then roll it up to make a cone.

✳ How to...

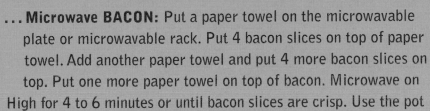

...Microwave BACON: Put a paper towel on the microwavable plate or microwavable rack. Put 4 bacon slices on top of paper towel. Add another paper towel and put 4 more bacon slices on top. Put one more paper towel on top of bacon. Microwave on High for 4 to 6 minutes or until bacon slices are crisp. Use the pot holders to take plate out of microwave.

Hot Dog Fold-Ups

Prep 15 minutes
Bake 15 minutes
Makes 8 roll-ups

Ingredients

1/4 cup (1/2 stick) butter or margarine

2 teaspoons yellow mustard

8 slices bread

4 slices (3/4 ounce each) American cheese

8 hot dogs

Ketchup or yellow mustard, if you like

Utensils

Table knife

Small saucepan (1 quart) or microwavable bowl and microwavable waxed paper

Wooden spoon

Measuring spoons

Cookie sheet

Pastry brush

Sharp knife

16 toothpicks

Pot holders

Pancake turner

1 Heat the oven to 375°F. Put the **BUTTER** in the saucepan. Heat butter over low heat for about 1 minute, stirring a few times with the wooden spoon, until it is melted. Take saucepan off hot burner. (Or put butter in the micro-wavable bowl. Cover bowl with microwavable waxed paper. Micro-wave butter on High for 30 to 45 seconds or until it is melted.) Stir in the **MUSTARD** until mixed.

2 Put the **BREAD** slices on the cookie sheet. Brush about half of the butter and mustard mixture over bread slices, using the pastry brush.

3 Cut the **CHEESE** slices in half on the cutting board, using the sharp knife, so you have 8 triangles. Put 1 cheese triangle on each slice of bread.

4 Put 1 of the **HOT DOGS** on each cheese triangle, using your fingers.

5 Fold each slice of bread over hot dog and cheese to make a triangle shape. Poke 2 toothpicks, one on each side, through bread and hot dog to keep everything together. Brush the outsides of the bread triangles with the rest of butter and mustard mixture.

6 Bake for 10 to 15 minutes or until bread is golden brown. Use the pot holders to take cookie sheet out of oven. Take the fold-ups off cookie sheet, using the pancake turner.

7 Remove the toothpicks from the fold-ups before eating. Serve fold-ups with the **KETCHUP** or **MUSTARD**, if you like.

1 Roll-Up: Calories 340 (Calories from Fat 240); Total Fat 26g (Saturated Fat 12g; Trans Fat 1g); Cholesterol 55mg; Sodium 1050mg; Total Carbohydrate 15g (Dietary Fiber 0g; Sugars 3g); Protein 10g
% Daily Value: Vitamin A 6%; Vitamin C 0%; Calcium 10%; Iron 8%   Exchanges: 1 Starch, 1 High-Fat Meat, 3 1/2 Fat   Carbohydrate Choices: 1

Chicken Lickin'

1 Cut the **CHICKEN** into bite-size pieces on the cutting board, using the sharp knife (or use the **CORN** or **TOMATOES**). Put the chicken (or corn or tomatoes) in the bowl. Add the **SALSA**. Stir with the wooden spoon until mixed.

Prep 15 minutes
Cook 4 minutes
Makes 4 quesadillas

Quesadillas

Ingredients

 Chef's Choice

1 package (6 ounces) refrigerated cooked Southwest-flavor chicken breast strips
or 1/2 cup frozen corn, thawed
or 1/2 cup chopped tomatoes

1/2 cup salsa
8 flour tortillas (6 to 8 inches in diameter)
Cooking spray
1 bag (8 ounces) finely shredded Colby-Monterey Jack cheese (2 cups)
1/4 cup sour cream, if you like
Extra salsa, if you like

Utensils

Cutting board
Sharp knife
Small mixing bowl
Liquid-ingredient measuring cup
Wooden spoon
Dry-ingredient measuring cups
Large nonstick skillet (10 inch)
Pancake turner
Pizza cutter

2 Spray 1 side of 1 **TORTILLA** with the **COOKING SPRAY**. Put the tortilla in the skillet, sprayed side down. Spoon about one-fourth of the salsa mixture on top of the tortilla in the skillet, and spread it with the back of the spoon. Sprinkle 1/2 cup of the **CHEESE** evenly over salsa mixture. Put another tortilla on top of the cheese. Spray the top of the quesadilla with cooking spray.

3 Cook over medium-high heat for about 2 minutes. Flip quesadilla over, using the pancake turner. Cook for about 2 minutes longer or until bottom tortilla is light golden brown and cheese is melted. Take quesadilla out of skillet, using pancake turner, and put it on cutting board. Repeat cooking the rest of the quesadillas.

4 Cut quesadillas into 6 triangles on the cutting board, using the pizza cutter or knife. Serve with **SOUR CREAM** and **EXTRA SALSA,** if you like.

1 Quesadilla: Calories 610 (Calories from Fat 280); Total Fat 31g (Saturated Fat 15g; Trans Fat 1.5g); Cholesterol 95mg; Sodium 1110mg; Total Carbohydrate 52g (Dietary Fiber 3g; Sugars 3g); Protein 31g
% Daily Value: Vitamin A 15%; Vitamin C 4%; Calcium 50%; Iron 20%
Exchanges: 3 1/2 Starch, 3 Lean Meat, 4 Fat Carbohydrate Choices: 3 1/2

Personal

Ingredients

1 English muffin
1 tablespoon pizza sauce
1 tablespoon shredded mozzarella cheese

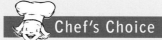 Chef's Choice

3 slices pepperoni
or 1 tablespoon diced cooked ham and
1 tablespoon pineapple tidbits
or 1 tablespoon frozen veggie
crumbles, thawed

Utensils

Table knife
Toaster
Measuring spoons
Microwavable paper towel
Microwavable plate or paper plate
Pot holders

1 Split the **ENGLISH MUFFIN** in half, using the table knife. Toast both halves in the toaster.

2 Top each toasted muffin half with the **PIZZA SAUCE** and **CHEESE**. Add the **PEPPERONI** (or **HAM** and **PINEAPPLE** or **VEGGIE CRUMBLES**).

3 Put the microwavable paper towel on the microwavable plate. Put muffin halves on paper towel.

4 Microwave on High for 30 to 45 seconds or until cheese is melted. Use the pot holders to take plate out of microwave. Cool pizzas about 2 minutes before eating.

2 Pizzas: Calories 230 (Calories from Fat 80); Total Fat 9g (Saturated Fat 3.5g; Trans Fat 0g); Cholesterol 25mg; Sodium 660mg; Total Carbohydrate 28g (Dietary Fiber 2g; Sugars 8g); Protein 10g   **% Daily Value:** Vitamin A 0%; Vitamin C 0%; Calcium 15%; Iron 10%   **Exchanges:** 1 1/2 Starch, 1/2 Other Carbohydrate, 1 High-Fat Meat   **Carbohydrate Choices:** 2

Pizzas

Prep 5 minutes
Microwave 45 seconds
Cool 2 minutes
Makes 2 pizzas

Chicken Caboodle Noodle Soup

Prep 10 minutes
Cook 15 minutes
Makes 4 servings

Ingredients

2 cans (14 ounces each) chicken broth

2 cups uncooked egg noodles or other pasta (4 ounces)

2 sprigs fresh parsley

1 cup cut-up cooked chicken

Crackers, if you like

Utensils

Can opener

Large saucepan with lid (3 quart)

Dry-ingredient measuring cups

Wooden spoon

Paper towels

Kitchen scissors

1  Open the cans of **CHICKEN BROTH** with the can opener. Pour broth into the saucepan. Cover saucepan with lid, and heat over medium-high heat until broth is boiling fast.

2 Add the **EGG NOODLES** to broth. Heat to boiling again. Boil uncovered for 6 to 8 minutes, stirring a few times with the wooden spoon, until noodles are soft but not mushy.

3 While the soup is cooking, rinse the **PARSLEY** in cool water. Pat dry with the paper towels. Cut parsley into small pieces, using the scissors.

4 Stir parsley and the **CHICKEN** into soup. Cook 1 to 2 minutes, stirring a few times, until chicken is hot. Serve soup with the **CRACKERS**, if you like.

1 Serving: Calories 200 (Calories from Fat 60); Total Fat 7g (Saturated Fat 2g; Trans Fat 0g); Cholesterol 55mg; Sodium 880mg; Total Carbohydrate 19g (Dietary Fiber 0g; Sugars 0g); Protein 17g   **% Daily Value:** Vitamin A 2%; Vitamin C 0%; Calcium 2%; Iron 10%   **Exchanges:** 1 Starch, 2 Lean Meat   **Carbohydrate Choices:** 1

Easy Mac and Cheese

Prep 5 minutes
Cook 25 minutes
Makes 4 servings

Ingredients

Water

2 cups uncooked elbow macaroni
or small pasta shells (about 8 ounces)

1 tablespoon butter or margarine

1 cup milk

1 1/2 cups shredded Cheddar cheese (6 ounces)
or 6 slices (1 ounce each) American cheese

1/2 teaspoon salt

1/2 teaspoon ground mustard

1/4 teaspoon pepper

Utensils

Large saucepan with lid (3 quart)

Dry-ingredient measuring cups

Wooden spoon

Colander

Pot holder

Liquid-ingredient measuring cup

Table knife

Measuring spoons

1 Fill the saucepan with **WATER** until it is about half full. Cover saucepan with lid, and heat over medium-high heat until water is boiling fast.

2 Add the **PASTA** to water. Heat to boiling again. Boil uncovered for 8 to 10 minutes, stirring often with the wooden spoon, until pasta is soft but not mushy. Drain pasta. ✱

3 Put drained pasta back into saucepan. Add the **BUTTER**, **MILK**, **CHEESE**, **SALT**, **MUSTARD** and **PEPPER** to pasta. Stir with spoon until mixed. Cook over low heat for about 5 minutes, stirring a few times, until cheese is melted.

✱ How to...

...**Drain Pasta:** Put a colander in the sink. Pour the pasta into the colander over the sink to drain. Don't forget to use a pot holder to hang on to the pot.

1 Serving: Calories 480 (Calories from Fat 180); Total Fat 19g (Saturated Fat 12g; Trans Fat 0.5g); Cholesterol 55mg; Sodium 610mg; Total Carbohydrate 54g (Dietary Fiber 4g; Sugars 5g); Protein 21g   **% Daily Value:** Vitamin A 15%; Vitamin C 0%; Calcium 30%; Iron 15%   **Exchanges:** 3 1/2 Starch, 1 1/2 High-Fat Meat, 1 Fat   **Carbohydrate Choices:** 3 1/2

Snacks & Drinks

Cheesy

Ingredients

Cooking spray

1 1/2 cups all-purpose flour

1/2 cup shredded Cheddar cheese (2 ounces)

2 tablespoons butter or margarine, softened

2 teaspoons baking powder

1 teaspoon sugar

1 teaspoon salt

2/3 cup milk

2 tablespoons all-purpose flour (to roll out dough)

1 egg

3 tablespoons coarse salt (not regular salt)

Utensils

Cookie sheet

Dry-ingredient measuring cups

Table knife

Liquid-ingredient measuring cup

Measuring spoons

Medium mixing bowl

Wooden spoon

Ruler, if you like

Small mixing bowl

Fork

Pastry brush

Pot holders

Pancake turner

Wire cooling rack

Pretzels

1 Heat the oven to 400°F. Spray the cookie sheet with the **COOKING SPRAY**. Put the 1 1/2 cups **FLOUR**, the **CHEESE**, **BUTTER**, **BAKING POWDER**, **SUGAR**, **SALT** and **MILK** in the medium bowl. Stir with the wooden spoon to make a soft dough.

2 Sprinkle the 2 tablespoons **FLOUR** over a clean work surface (such as the kitchen counter or a large cutting board). Put dough on surface. Divide dough in half to make 2 balls. Roll each ball of dough around 3 or 4 times. Knead the dough 10 times. ✳

3 Divide each ball of dough into 8 pieces. Roll each piece into a 12-inch rope. Use the ruler to measure, if you like. To shape each pretzel, shape the rope into a circle, overlapping rope about 2 inches from each end, leaving the ends of the rope free. Take 1 end in each hand; twist once where rope crosses. Lift ends over to opposite side of circle. Pinch ends to seal. Put pretzels on cookie sheet.

4 Crack the **EGG** on side of the small bowl, letting egg slip into bowl. Beat egg with the fork until the yolk and white are mixed. Brush egg over pretzels, using the pastry brush. Sprinkle about 1/2 teaspoon **SALT** on each pretzel.

5 Bake for 15 to 20 minutes or until pretzels are golden brown. Use the pot holders to take cookie sheet out of oven. Take pretzels off cookie sheet, using the pancake turner. Place pretzels on the wire cooling rack. Cool for about 3 minutes before eating.

✳ How to...

...Knead Dough: Curve your fingers around and fold the dough toward you. Push the dough away from you with the heels of your hands, using a quick rocking motion. The dough should look smooth and stretchy when you're done.

1 Pretzel: Calories 90 (Calories from Fat 30); Total Fat 3.5g (Saturated Fat 2g; Trans Fat 0g); Cholesterol 20mg; Sodium 1580mg; Total Carbohydrate 11g (Dietary Fiber 0g; Sugars 0g); Protein 3g   **% Daily Value:** Vitamin A 2%; Vitamin C 0%; Calcium 6%; Iron 4%   **Exchanges:** 1 Starch, 1/2 Fat Carbohydrate Choices: 1

Pizza

Prep 5 minutes
Microwave 45 seconds
Makes 2 pizza sticks

Sticks

Ingredients

2 soft breadsticks or bagel sticks
2 tablespoons pizza sauce

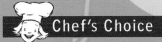 Chef's Choice

10 thin slices pepperoni
or 1 tablespoon chopped green olives
or 4 small slices cooked chicken,
cut into strips

1 stick string cheese

Utensils

Cutting board
Sharp knife
Measuring spoons
Table knife
Microwavable plate
Microwavable paper towel
Pot holders

1 Place the **BREADSTICKS** on their sides on the cutting board. Cut each breadstick lengthwise almost in half (not all the way through), using the sharp knife. Open breadsticks (the top and bottom halves should still be connected on one long side).

2 Spread half (1 tablespoon) of the **PIZZA SAUCE** on the inside of each breadstick, using the table knife.

3 Put 5 slices of **PEPPERONI** (or half of the **GREEN OLIVES** or half of the **CHICKEN**) on the bottom half of each breadstick. Overlap the pepperoni slices so they fit.

4 Tear the **STRING CHEESE** in half. Put half on one breadstick and the other half on the other breadstick.

5 Close breadsticks. Put breadsticks on the microwavable plate and cover with the microwavable paper towel. Microwave breadsticks on High for **15 to 45** seconds or until warm. Use the pot holders to take plate out of microwave.

1 Pizza Stick: Calories 260 (Calories from Fat 140); Total Fat 15g (Saturated Fat 6g; Trans Fat 0g); Cholesterol 40mg; Sodium 820mg; Total Carbohydrate 19g (Dietary Fiber 2g; Sugars 1g); Protein 12g % Daily Value: Vitamin A 0%; Vitamin C 0%; Calcium 15%; Iron 10% Exchanges: 1 1/2 Starch, 1 High-Fat Meat, 1 Fat Carbohydrate Choices: 1

Ants

Ingredients

4 medium stalks celery

1/2 cup peanut butter

Raisins or dried fruit pieces

Prep 10 minutes

Makes 12 "logs"

On a Log

Utensils

Paper towels
Cutting board
Sharp knife

Dry-ingredient
measuring cup
Table knife

1 Wash the **CELERY** in cool water. Pat dry with the paper towels. Cut the leafy end off celery on the cutting board, using the sharp knife. Cut each celery stalk into 3 pieces.

2 Spread the U shaped part of each celery piece with the **PEANUT BUTTER**, using the table knife. Press the **RAISINS** into peanut butter.

3 "logs": Calories 250 (Calories from Fat 150); Total Fat 17g (Saturated Fat 3.5g; Trans Fat 0g); Cholesterol 0mg; Sodium 190mg; Total Carbohydrate 15g (Dietary Fiber 3g, Sugars 9g); Protein 9g   % Daily Value: Vitamin A 4%; Vitamin C 2%; Calcium 4%; Iron 4%   Exchanges: 1/2 Other Carbohydrate, 1 Vegetable, 1 High-Fat Meat, 2 Fat   Carbohydrate Choices: 1

Super Supreme

Prep 10 minutes
Bake 4 minutes
Makes 5 servings

Ingredients

25 tortilla chips

1/4 cup salsa

Chef's Choice

1 cup shredded Cheddar cheese (4 ounces)
or 1 cup shredded Monterey
Jack cheese (4 ounces)
or 1 cup shredded Mexican cheese
blend (4 ounces)

Extra salsa, if you like

Utensils

Cookie sheet
Foil
Liquid-ingredient measuring cup
Spoon
Dry-ingredient measuring cups
Pot holders

Nachos

1 Heat the oven to 400°F. Cover the cookie sheet with the foil.

2 Put the **TORTILLA CHIPS** on foil-lined cookie sheet. Spoon the **SALSA** over tortilla chips so each chip has some salsa on it. Sprinkle the **CHEDDAR CHEESE** (or **MONTEREY JACK** or **MEXICAN**) evenly on top of salsa and chips.

3 Bake for about 4 minutes or until cheese is melted. Use the pot holders to take cookie sheet out of oven.

4 Serve the nachos with the **EXTRA SALSA**, if you like.

1 Serving: Calories 140 (Calories from Fat 90); Total Fat 10g (Saturated Fat 5g; Trans Fat 0g); Cholesterol 25mg; Sodium 250mg; Total Carbohydrate 7g (Dietary Fiber 0g; Sugars 0g); Protein 6g   **% Daily Value:** Vitamin A 6%; Vitamin C 0%; Calcium 15%; Iron 4%   **Exchanges:** 1/2 Starch, 1/2 High-Fat Meat, 1 Fat   **Carbohydrate Choices:** 1/2

Chex® "Snax"

Ingredients

3 tablespoons butter or margarine

3/4 teaspoon seasoned salt

1/4 to 1/2 teaspoon garlic powder

1/4 teaspoon onion powder

1 tablespoon Worcestershire sauce

1 1/2 cups Corn Chex® cereal

1 1/2 cups Rice Chex® cereal

1 1/2 cups Wheat Chex® cereal

1/2 cup mixed nuts

1/2 cup small pretzel twists

1/2 cup miniature or regular-size garlic-flavored bagel chips (break regular-size ones into 1-inch pieces)

Utensils

Table knife

Large microwavable bowl

Pot holders

Measuring spoons

Wooden spoon

Dry-ingredient measuring cups

Paper towels

Plastic bag with zipper top or airtight container

Prep 15 minutes

Microwave 5 minutes 30 seconds

Makes 6 cups

-TRIP-

1 Put the **BUTTER** in the bowl. Microwave on High for 20 to 30 seconds or until butter is melted. Use the pot holders to take bowl out of microwave.

2 Add the **SEASONED SALT**, **GARLIC POWDER** (if you like the taste of garlic, use the larger amount), **ONION POWDER** and **WORCESTERSHIRE SAUCE** to butter. Stir with the wooden spoon until mixed. Add all 3 of the **CEREALS**, the **NUTS**, **PRETZELS** and **BAGEL CHIPS**. Carefully stir until all ingredients are coated with butter mixture.

3 Microwave on High for 3 to 5 minutes, carefully stirring every minute. Use the pot holders to take bowl out of microwave. Spread the "snax" on the paper towels. Let it cool until no longer warm when touched. Store "snax" in the plastic bag or airtight container.

1/2 Cup: Calories 130 (Calories from Fat 60); Total Fat 7g (Saturated Fat 2.5g; Trans Fat 0g); Cholesterol 10mg; Sodium 310mg; Total Carbohydrate 15g (Dietary Fiber 2g; Sugars 2g); Protein 3g   % Daily Value: Vitamin A 6%; Vitamin C 0%; Calcium 4%; Iron 25%   Exchanges: 1 Starch, 1 Fat Carbohydrate Choices: 1

Ingredients

6 cups popped popcorn (about 1/4 cup unpopped)

1/2 cup packed brown sugar

1/4 cup (1/2 stick) butter or margarine

2 tablespoons light corn syrup

1/4 teaspoon salt

1/4 teaspoon baking soda

Prep 15 minutes
Cook 8 minutes
Bake 1 hour
Cool 15 minutes
Makes about 6 cups

LOO

Utensils

Dry-ingredient measuring cups

Rectangular pan (13 × 9 inch)

Measuring spoons

Medium saucepan (2 quart)

Wooden spoon

Pot holders

Airtight container

1 Cup: Calories 240 (Calories from Fat 110); Total Fat 13g (Saturated Fat 6g; Trans Fat 0g); Cholesterol 20mg; Sodium 220mg; Total Carbohydrate 30g (Dietary Fiber 1g; Sugars 20g); Protein 1g **% Daily Value:** Vitamin A 6%; Vitamin C 0%; Calcium 0%; Iron 4% **Exchanges:** 1/2 Starch, 1 1/2 Other Carbohydrate, 2 1/2 Fat **Carbohydrate Choices:** 2

Caramel Corn Commotion

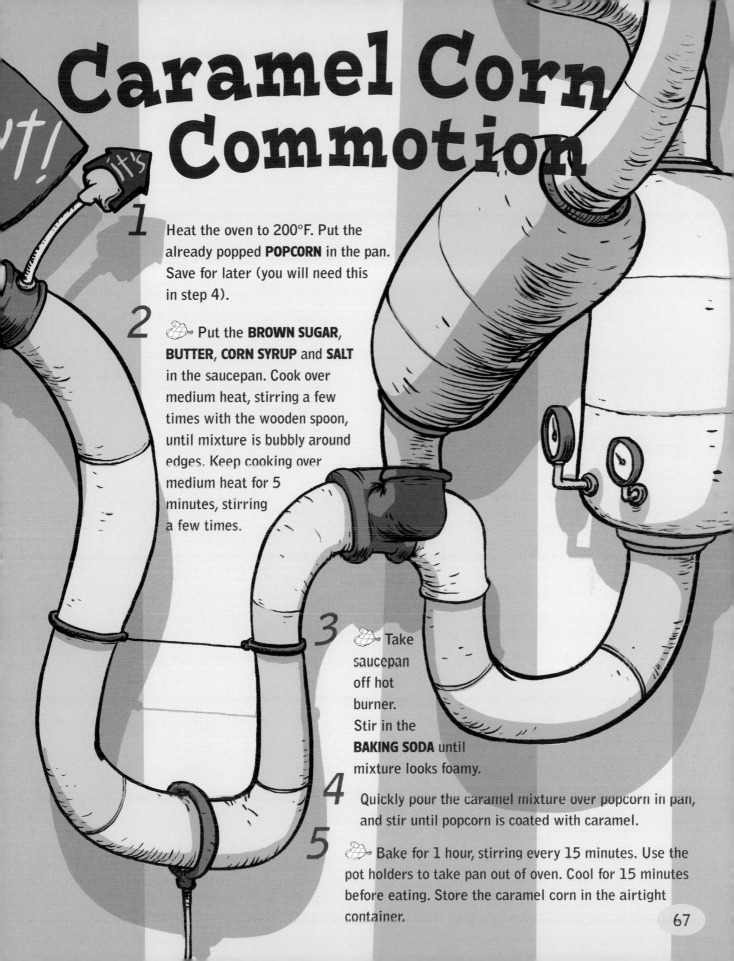

1 Heat the oven to 200°F. Put the already popped **POPCORN** in the pan. Save for later (you will need this in step 4).

2 Put the **BROWN SUGAR**, **BUTTER**, **CORN SYRUP** and **SALT** in the saucepan. Cook over medium heat, stirring a few times with the wooden spoon, until mixture is bubbly around edges. Keep cooking over medium heat for 5 minutes, stirring a few times.

3 Take saucepan off hot burner. Stir in the **BAKING SODA** until mixture looks foamy.

4 Quickly pour the caramel mixture over popcorn in pan, and stir until popcorn is coated with caramel.

5 Bake for 1 hour, stirring every 15 minutes. Use the pot holders to take pan out of oven. Cool for 15 minutes before eating. Store the caramel corn in the airtight container.

67

Fantastic Dip 'n' Fruit

Prep 15 minutes
Makes 10 servings

Ingredients

2 containers (6 oz each) vanilla
thick-and-creamy low-fat yogurt

1 tablespoon packed brown sugar

1/4 teaspoon ground cinnamon

Dash of nutmeg

1/2 of a honeydew melon

1/4 of a cantaloupe

10 raspberries (1/3 cup)

boing

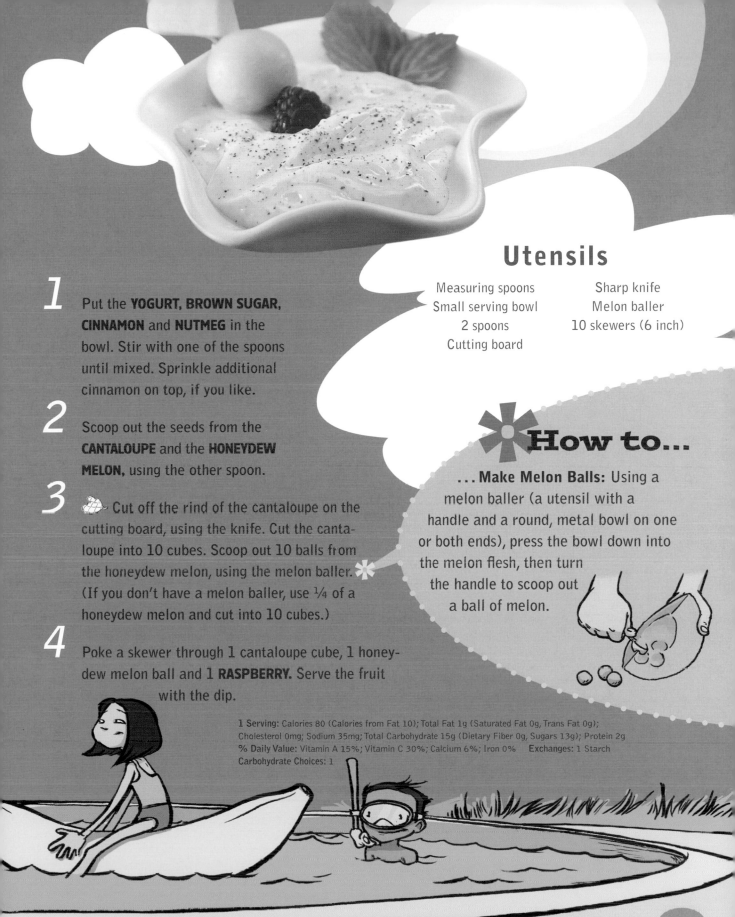

1 Put the **YOGURT, BROWN SUGAR, CINNAMON** and **NUTMEG** in the bowl. Stir with one of the spoons until mixed. Sprinkle additional cinnamon on top, if you like.

2 Scoop out the seeds from the **CANTALOUPE** and the **HONEYDEW MELON,** using the other spoon.

3 Cut off the rind of the cantaloupe on the cutting board, using the knife. Cut the cantaloupe into 10 cubes. Scoop out 10 balls from the honeydew melon, using the melon baller. (If you don't have a melon baller, use ¼ of a honeydew melon and cut into 10 cubes.)

4 Poke a skewer through 1 cantaloupe cube, 1 honeydew melon ball and 1 **RASPBERRY.** Serve the fruit with the dip.

Utensils

Measuring spoons
Small serving bowl
2 spoons
Cutting board

Sharp knife
Melon baller
10 skewers (6 inch)

How to...

...Make Melon Balls: Using a melon baller (a utensil with a handle and a round, metal bowl on one or both ends), press the bowl down into the melon flesh, then turn the handle to scoop out a ball of melon.

1 Serving: Calories 80 (Calories from Fat 10); Total Fat 1g (Saturated Fat 0g, Trans Fat 0g); Cholesterol 0mg; Sodium 35mg; Total Carbohydrate 15g (Dietary Fiber 0g, Sugars 13g); Protein 2g % Daily Value: Vitamin A 15%; Vitamin C 30%; Calcium 6%; Iron 0% Exchanges: 1 Starch Carbohydrate Choices: 1

Fresh

Ingredients

3 large tomatoes
1 small green bell pepper
8 medium green onions
Fresh cilantro
3 cloves garlic
2 to 3 tablespoons lime juice
1/2 teaspoon salt

Utensils

Paper towels
Cutting board
Sharp knife
Dry-ingredient measuring cups
Kitchen scissors
Measuring spoons
Garlic press, if you like
Large glass or plastic serving bowl
Plastic wrap

Prep 20 minutes
Makes 3 1/2 cups

Tomato Salsa

1 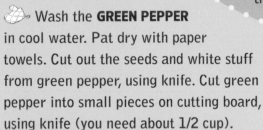 Wash the **TOMATOES** in cool water. Pat dry with the paper towels. Remove the seeds from the tomatoes. ✳ Cut the tomato halves into small pieces on cutting board, using knife (you need about 3 cups).

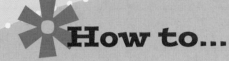

✳ How to...

. . . **Seed Tomatoes:** Cut each tomato horizontally (right to left, not top to bottom) in half on the cutting board, using the knife. Squeeze each tomato half over the sink to get the seeds out.

2 Wash the **GREEN PEPPER** in cool water. Pat dry with paper towels. Cut out the seeds and white stuff from green pepper, using knife. Cut green pepper into small pieces on cutting board, using knife (you need about 1/2 cup).

3 Peel off the outside layer of the **GREEN ONIONS.** Slice onions into small pieces on cutting board with knife (you need about 1/2 cup).

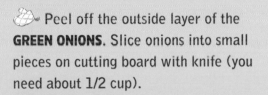

4 Rinse the **CILANTRO** in cool water. Pat dry with paper towels. Cut cilantro into small pieces, using the scissors (you need about 2 tablespoons).

5 Take the papery layer off the cloves of **GARLIC.** Cut garlic into tiny pieces on cutting board, using knife. You can use a garlic press instead, if you like.

6 Put tomatoes, green pepper, onions, cilantro, and garlic in the serving bowl. Add the **LIME JUICE** and **SALT**. Stir with the wooden spoon until mixed. Cover bowl with the plastic wrap. Put bowl in the refrigerator until you are ready to serve the salsa.

1/4 Cup: Calories 15 (Calories from Fat 0); Total Fat 0g (Saturated Fat 0g; Trans Fat 0g); Cholesterol 0mg; Sodium 90mg; Total Carbohydrate 3g (Dietary Fiber 0g; Sugars 2g); Protein 0g   **% Daily Value:** Vitamin A 8%; Vitamin C 20%; Calcium 0%; Iron 0%   **Exchanges:** Free   Carbohydrate Choices: 0

Pucker-Up Lemonade

Ingredients

4 lemons

3 cups water

1/2 cup sugar

Ice cubes

Lemon or orange slices, if you like

Utensils

Cutting board

Sharp knife

Small mixing bowl

Juicer, if you like

Liquid-ingredient measuring cup

Large pitcher

Dry-ingredient measuring cups

Wooden spoon

6 drinking glasses

1 Roll a **LEMON** back and forth on the counter with the palm of your hand (it helps if lemons are room temperature). Cut lemon horizontally in half on the cutting board, using the knife. Squeeze each lemon half over the bowl, using your hands or a juicer to get the juice out. Repeat with the rest of the lemons until you have 1 cup of lemon juice. Remove any seeds that might be in the juice.

2 Pour lemon juice into the pitcher. Add the **WATER** and **SUGAR**. Stir with the wooden spoon until mixed.

3 Put a few **ICE CUBES** in each of the drinking glasses. Pour the lemonade into glasses. Put a **LEMON SLICE** in each glass, if you like.

1 Serving: Calories 80 (Calories from Fat 0); Total Fat 0g (Saturated Fat 0g; Trans Fat 0g); Cholesterol 0mg; Sodium 10mg; Total Carbohydrate 19g (Dietary Fiber 0g; Sugars 18g); Protein 0g **% Daily Value:** Vitamin A 0%; Vitamin C 15%; Calcium 0%; Iron 0% **Exchanges:** 1 1/2 Other Carbohydrate **Carbohydrate Choices:** 1

Purple Cow Shakes

Prep 5 minutes
Makes 4 shakes

74

Ingredients

1 can (6 ounces) frozen grape juice concentrate
1 cup milk
2 cups vanilla ice cream

1 Put the **GRAPE JUICE CONCENTRATE** and **MILK** in the blender.

2 Add the **ICE CREAM** to the grape juice mixture.

3 Cover blender with lid, and blend on high speed 30 seconds. Pour the shake into the drinking glasses, and serve right away.

1 Shake: Calories 260 (Calories from Fat 80); Total Fat 9g (Saturated Fat 6g; Trans Fat 0g); Cholesterol 35mg; Sodium 85mg; Total Carbohydrate 39g (Dietary Fiber 0g; Sugars 34g); Protein 5g **% Daily Value:** Vitamin A 8%; Vitamin C 60%; Calcium 15%; Iron 0% **Exchanges:** 1 Fruit, 1 Other Carbohydrate, 1/2 Low-Fat Milk, 1 1/2 Fat **Carbohydrate Choices:** 2 1/2

Utensils

Liquid-ingredient measuring cup
Blender with lid
Ice cream scoop or large spoon
Dry-ingredient measuring cups
4 drinking glasses

On The Side

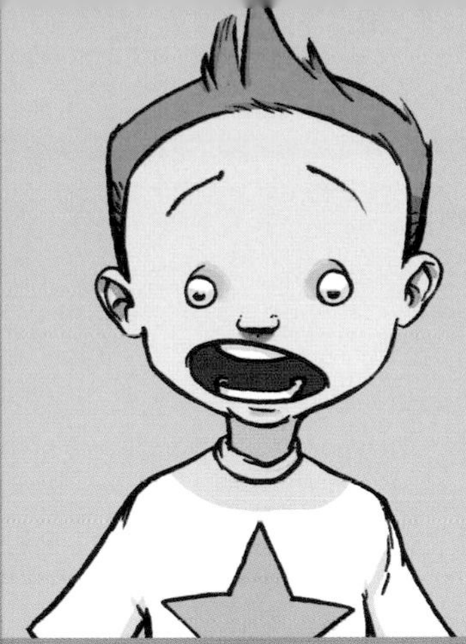

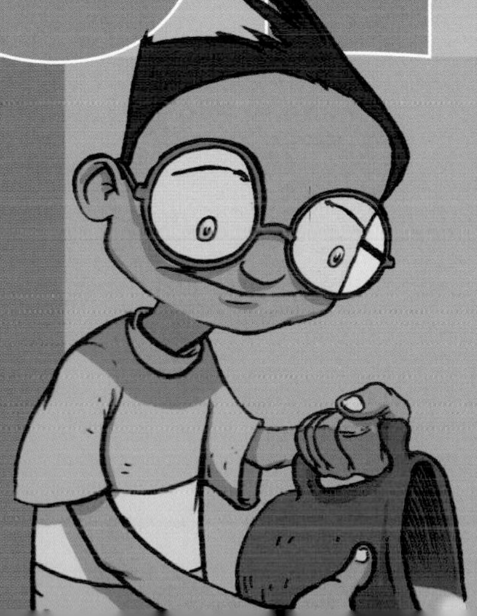

Caesar Salad

Ingredients

1 large or 2 small bunches romaine lettuce
1/2 cup Caesar dressing
1 cup Caesar- or garlic-flavored croutons
1/3 cup finely shredded Parmesan cheese
(1 1/3 ounces)
Coarse ground black pepper

Utensils

Paper towels
Dry-ingredient measuring cups
Liquid-ingredient measuring cup
Large salad bowl
Wooden spoon

1 Wash the **LETTUCE** in cool water. Pat dry with the paper towels. Tear lettuce into bite-size pieces (you need about 10 cups).

2 Pour the **CAESAR DRESSING** into the bowl. Add lettuce. Stir with the wooden spoon until lettuce gets coated with dressing. Sprinkle the **CROUTONS**, **CHEESE** and **PEPPER** over salad. Stir with the spoon until mixed.

1 Serving: Calories 170 (Calories from Fat 120); Total Fat 14g (Saturated Fat 3g; Trans Fat 0g); Cholesterol 5mg; Sodium 350mg; Total Carbohydrate 7g (Dietary Fiber 2g; Sugars 1g); Protein 4g **% Daily Value:** Vitamin A 100%; Vitamin C 35%; Calcium 10%; Iron 6%   **Exchanges:** 1 Vegetable, 3 Fat   **Carbohydrate Choices:** 1/2

Pasta Tubes and Tomato Salad

Ingredients

Water

1 1/2 cups uncooked penne pasta
(6 ounces)

 Chef's Choice

1/4 cup vinaigrette
(oil and vinegar dressing)
OR 1/4 cup ranch dressing
OR 1/4 cup Italian dressing

1 small red tomato
1 small yellow tomato
2 tablespoons finely
shredded Parmesan cheese

Utensils

Medium saucepan with lid
(2 quart)
Dry-ingredient measuring cups
Wooden spoon
Colander
Large serving bowl
Liquid-ingredient measuring
cup
Plastic wrap
Paper towels
Cutting board
Sharp knife
Measuring spoons

Prep 5 minutes
Cook 20 minutes
Chill 2 hours
Makes 4 or 5 servings

1 Fill the saucepan with **WATER** until it is about half full. Cover saucepan with lid, and heat over medium-high heat until water is boiling fast.

2  Add the **PASTA** to water. Heat to boiling again. Boil uncovered for 8 to 10 minutes, stirring often with the wooden spoon, until pasta is soft but not mushy. Pour pasta into the colander over the sink to drain. Rinse pasta with cold water until no longer warm when touched.

3 Put the drained pasta in the bowl. Add half (2 tablespoons) of the **VINAIGRETTE** (or **RANCH DRESSING** or **ITALIAN DRESSING**) to bowl. Stir with spoon until mixed. Cover bowl with the plastic wrap, and put in the refrigerator for 2 hours or until you are ready to eat it.

4 Wash the **TOMATOES** in cool water. Pat dry with the paper towels. Cut tomatoes into wedges on the cutting board, using the knife.

5 When you are ready to eat, take plastic wrap off bowl. Add tomatoes and the rest of the **VINAIGRETTE** (or **RANCH** or **ITALIAN DRESSING**) to pasta. Stir with spoon until mixed. Sprinkle the **CHEESE** over the top.

1 Serving: Calories 230 (Calories from Fat 80); Total Fat 9g (Saturated Fat 1.5g; Trans Fat 0g); Cholesterol 40mg; Sodium 190mg; Total Carbohydrate 31g (Dietary Fiber 2g; Sugars 3g); Protein 7g   % Daily Value: Vitamin A 8%; Vitamin C 10%; Calcium 6%; Iron 10%   Exchanges: 2 Starch, 1 1/2 Fat   Carbohydrate Choices: 2

Prep 10 minutes
Makes 4 servings

Easy

Ingredients

1 can (11 ounces) mandarin orange segments, chilled

1 can (8 ounces) pineapple chunks in syrup, chilled

1 red apple

1 container (6 ounces) plain yogurt (about 2/3 cup)

1 tablespoon honey

1 tablespoon lemon juice

1 cup seedless grapes

1 cup torn (into bite-size pieces) salad greens

Utensils

Can opener

Colander

Paper towels

Cutting board

Sharp knife

Dry-ingredient measuring cups

Measuring spoons

Medium mixing bowl

Wooden spoon

1 Open the can of **ORANGES** and the can of **PINEAPPLE** with the can opener. Pour both cans into the colander over the sink to drain.

2 Wash the **APPLE** in cool water. Pat dry with the paper towels. Cut apple into 4 sections on the cutting board, using the knife. Cut out the apple core and seeds. Cut the apple sections into slices (you need about 1 cup).

3 Put the **YOGURT**, **HONEY** and **LEMON JUICE** in the bowl. Stir with the wooden spoon until mixed. Add the drained oranges, pineapple, apple, **GRAPES** and **SALAD GREENS** to the yogurt mixture. Stir with the spoon until mixed.

1 Serving: Calories 160 (Calories from Fat 10); Total Fat 1g (Saturated Fat 0g; Trans Fat 0g); Cholesterol 0mg; Sodium 35mg; Total Carbohydrate 34g (Dietary Fiber 3g; Sugars 30g); Protein 3g   **% Daily Value:** Vitamin A 20%; Vitamin C 60%; Calcium 10%; Iron 4%   **Exchanges:** 1 Fruit, 1 Other Carbohydrate, 1/2 Skim Milk   **Carbohydrate Choices:** 2

Prep 20 minutes
Microwave 8 minutes
Cook 8 minutes
Makes 6 servings

Trees

Ingredients

1 1/2 pounds fresh broccoli

3 tablespoons water

6 ounces process American cheese loaf

1/3 cup milk

1/4 teaspoon onion salt

1 drop red pepper sauce, if you like

1 Serving: Calories 140 (Calories from Fat 80); Total Fat 9g (Saturated Fat 6g; Trans Fat 0g); Cholesterol 30mg; Sodium 520mg; Total Carbohydrate 6g (Dietary Fiber 2g; Sugars 2g); Protein 9g   **% Daily Value:** Vitamin A 15%; Vitamin C 50%; Calcium 20%; Iron 4%   **Exchanges:** 1 Vegetable, 1 High-Fat Meat   **Carbohydrate Choices:** 1/2

84

with Cheese

Utensils

Paper towels
Cutting board
Sharp knife
Measuring spoons
Medium microwavable bowl
Microwavable plastic wrap
Liquid-ingredient measuring cup
Medium saucepan (2 quart)
Wooden spoon
Pot holders
Colander
Medium serving bowl

1 Rinse the **BROCCOLI** in cool water. Pat dry with the paper towels. Tear off any outside leaves from broccoli. Cut off the hard ends of the stems on the cutting board, using the knife. Cut broccoli into small tree-like pieces.

2 Put the broccoli and **WATER** in the microwavable bowl. Cover bowl with the microwavable plastic wrap. Fold one of the edges of plastic wrap back about 1/4 inch (this lets the steam out when you microwave it). Microwave on High for 6 to 8 minutes or until broccoli is hot and crisp-tender.

3 While broccoli is cooking in microwave, cut the **CHEESE** into small pieces on cutting board, using knife. Put the cheese, **MILK**, **ONION SALT** and **RED PEPPER SAUCE** (if you like) in the saucepan. Heat over medium heat for 6 to 8 minutes, stirring all the time with the wooden spoon, until cheese is melted and mixture is smooth.

4 Use the pot holders to take bowl out of microwave. Pour broccoli into the colander over the sink to drain. Put broccoli in the serving bowl. Pour hot cheese over broccoli.

Garlic Oven Fries

Ingredients

Cooking spray
4 medium red potatoes (2 1/2 to 3 inch)
2 teaspoons olive or vegetable oil
1 teaspoon dried basil leaves
1 teaspoon garlic salt

Utensils

Rectangular pan with sides
(15 × 10 inch)
Vegetable brush
Cutting board
Sharp knife
Medium mixing bowl
Measuring spoons
Wooden spoon
Pot holders

Prep 10 minutes
Bake 18 minutes
Makes 4 servings

1 Heat the oven to 500°F. Spray the pan with the **COOKING SPRAY**.

2 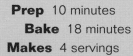 Scrub the **POTATOES** with the vegetable brush. Cut each potato lengthwise into 8 wedges on the cutting board, using the knife. Put potatoes in the bowl.

3 Drizzle the **OLIVE OIL** over potatoes. Toss potatoes with the wooden spoon to coat them with oil. Sprinkle potatoes with the **BASIL** and **GARLIC SALT**. ✳ Spread potatoes in a single layer in pan.

4 Bake for 8 minutes. Stir potatoes with spoon and bake for 7 to 10 minutes longer or until they are a little soft but crisp on the outside. Use the pot holders to take pan out of oven.

✳ How to...

...Use Fresh Herbs: If you (or someone you know) grow basil, you can use fresh basil instead of dried. Just pluck the leaves from the plant and cut them into tiny pieces with a sharp knife. Because you're using fresh herbs instead of dried, you need 1 tablespoon instead of 1 teaspoon.

PICK

1 Serving: Calories 190 (Calories from Fat 30); Total Fat 3g (Saturated Fat 0g; Trans Fat 0g); Cholesterol 0mg; Sodium 260mg; Total Carbohydrate 37g (Dietary Fiber 4g; Sugars 2g); Protein 4g   **% Daily Value:** Vitamin A 0%; Vitamin C 15%; Calcium 4%; Iron 10%   **Exchanges:** 2 Starch, 1/2 Fat **Carbohydrate Choices:** 2 1/2

Mash 'em Smash 'em

Ingredients

6 medium potatoes (about 2 pounds total)

2 1/2 cups water

1/2 cup milk

1/4 cup (1/2 stick) butter or margarine, softened

Chef's Choice

1/4 cup shredded Cheddar cheese (1 ounce)

or 1 tablespoon chopped chives

or 2 tablespoons bacon-flavor bits or chips

1/2 teaspoon salt

1/8 teaspoon pepper

Prep 20 minutes
Cook 30 minutes
Makes 6 servings

Potatoes

Utensils

Vegetable brush
Vegetable peeler
Cutting board
Sharp knife
Liquid-ingredient measuring cup
Large saucepan with lid (3 quart)
Fork
Colander
Potato masher
Measuring spoons
Wooden spoon

1 Scrub the **POTATOES** in cool water with the vegetable brush. Peel skins from potatoes, using the vegetable peeler.

2 Cut potatoes into large pieces on the cutting board, using the knife.

3 Pour the **WATER** into the saucepan. Cover saucepan with lid, and heat over medium-high heat until water is boiling fast.

4 Add potatoes to water. Cover saucepan with lid, and heat to boiling. When water is boiling, turn the heat down just enough so water bubbles gently. Cook saucepan again with lid, and cook 20 to 25 minutes or until potatoes are soft when poked with the fork.

5 Take saucepan off hot burner. Dump potatoes into the colander over the sink to drain. Put potatoes back in saucepan. Shake saucepan gently over low heat until water has disappeared.

6 Mash potatoes with the potato masher until smooth and no lumps are left. Add the **MILK**, a little at a time, and mash some more.

7 Add the **BUTTER**, **CHEESE** (or **CHIVES** or **BACON BITS**), **SALT** and **PEPPER** to potatoes. Stir with the wooden spoon until mixed.

1 Serving: Calories 220 (Calories from Fat 90); Total Fat 10g (Saturated Fat 6g; Trans Fat 0.5g); Cholesterol 25mg; Sodium 300mg; Total Carbohydrate 28g (Dietary Fiber 3g; Sugars 2g); Protein 4g   % Daily Value: Vitamin A 6%; Vitamin C 8%; Calcium 6%; Iron 2%   **Exchanges:** 2 Starch, 1 1/2 Fat   **Carbohydrate Choices:** 2

Fried Rice

Ingredients

1 cup uncooked regular long-grain rice
2 cups water
1 cup bean sprouts
2 medium green onions with tops
1 tablespoon vegetable oil
2 eggs
1 tablespoon vegetable oil
3 tablespoons soy sauce
Dash of pepper

Prep 25 minutes
Cook 20 minutes
Makes 4 servings

Utensils

Dry-ingredient measuring cups
Liquid-ingredient measuring cup
Medium saucepan with lid (2 quart)
Wooden spoon
Colander
Cutting board
Sharp knife
Measuring spoons
Large skillet (10 inch)
Small mixing bowl
Fork

1 Put the **RICE** and **WATER** in the saucepan. Heat over high heat, stirring a few times with the wooden spoon to keep rice from sticking. When water is boiling fast, turn down the heat just a little so water bubbles gently. Cover saucepan with lid, and cook for about 15 minutes or until rice is fluffy and tender.

2 While rice is cooking, continue with the recipe. (If the rice is done before you need it, take saucepan off hot burner, and let it sit a few minutes until you're ready to use it.)

3 Put the **BEAN SPROUTS** into the colander over the sink, and rinse with cool water. Let them drain in sink. Peel off the outside layer of the **GREEN ONIONS**. Slice the green onions into small pieces on the cutting board, using the knife.

4 Put the first 1 tablespoon **VEGETABLE OIL** in the skillet. Heat over medium heat for 1 to 2 minutes. (To test skillet, sprinkle with a few drops of water. If bubbles jump around, the oil is heated just right.)

5 Add bean sprouts, onions and cooked rice to skillet. Cook until hot, stirring all the time with spoon. Take skillet off hot burner.

6 Crack the **EGGS** on side of the bowl, letting eggs slip into bowl. Beat eggs slightly, using the fork. Push rice mixture to one side of skillet with spoon. Add the second 1 tablespoon **VEGETABLE OIL** to the open spot, then pour eggs into this spot. Cook over medium heat, stirring eggs all the time with spoon, until they are slightly firm but not runny.

7 Stir eggs and rice mixture together with spoon until mixed. Stir in the **SOY SAUCE** and **PEPPER**.

1 Serving: Calories 310 (Calories from Fat 100); Total Fat 11g (Saturated Fat 2g; Trans Fat 0g); Cholesterol 105mg; Sodium 720mg; Total Carbohydrate 43g (Dietary Fiber 0g; Sugars 1g); Protein 10g   % Daily Value: Vitamin A 4%; Vitamin C 4%; Calcium 4%; Iron 15%   Exchanges: 3 Starch, 2 Fat   Carbohydrate Choices: 3

Garlic

Bread

Ingredients

1/3 cup butter or margarine, softened

1/4 teaspoon garlic powder

1 loaf (1 pound) French bread

Prep 10 minutes
Bake 20 minutes
Makes 1 loaf (18 slices)

Utensils

Measuring spoons
Small mixing bowl
Wooden spoon
Cutting board
Serrated knife
Table knife
Heavy-duty foil
Pot holders

1 Heat the oven to 400°F.

2 Put the **BUTTER** and **GARLIC POWDER** in the bowl. Stir with the wooden spoon until mixed.

3 Cut the **BREAD** into 1-inch-thick slices on the cutting board, using the serrated knife. Spread butter mixture over 1 side of each slice of bread, using the table knife. Put the loaf back together, and wrap it up tight in a sheet of the foil that is about 4 inches longer than the loaf of bread.

4 Bake for 15 to 20 minutes or until bread is hot. Use the pot holders to take bread out of oven. Carefully unwrap bread. It will be hot!

1 Slice: Calories 100 (Calories from Fat 40); Total Fat 4.5g (Saturated Fat 2.5g; Trans Fat 0g); Cholesterol 10mg; Sodium 170mg; Total Carbohydrate 13g (Dietary Fiber 0g; Sugars 0g); Protein 2g   % Daily Value: Vitamin A 2%; Vitamin C 0%; Calcium 2%; Iron 4%   Exchanges: 1 Starch, 1 Fat   Carbohydrate Choices: 1

Time for Dinner

Mini Meat Loaves

Prep 5 minutes
Bake 25 minutes
Makes 4 servings

Ingredients

1 small onion
1 pound lean ground beef
1/2 cup plain dry bread crumbs
1/4 cup milk
1/2 teaspoon salt
1/4 teaspoon pepper
1/2 teaspoon Worcestershire sauce, if you like
1 egg

Utensils

Paper towel

Cutting board

Sharp knife

Dry-ingredient measuring cups

Liquid-ingredient measuring cup

Measuring spoons

Large mixing bowl

Wooden spoon

Rectangular glass baking dish (13 × 9 inch; 3 quart)

Ruler

Table knife

Meat thermometer

Pot holders

Pancake turner

1 Peel the outside layer of skin from the **ONION**. Wash onion in cool water. Pat dry with the paper towel. Cut onion into very small pieces on the cutting board, using the sharp knife (you need about 1/4 cup).

2 Heat the oven to 400°F. Put the onion, **GROUND BEEF, BREAD CRUMBS, MILK, SALT, PEPPER** and **WORCESTERSHIRE SAUCE** (if you like) in the bowl. Crack the **EGG** on side of bowl, letting egg slip into bowl. Stir with the wooden spoon until mixed.

3 Put the mixture in the baking dish. Shape mixture into 9 × 3-inch rectangle, using your hands (use the ruler to measure). Cut mixture in half the long way, using the table knife. Cut into 4 rows the short way. You should wind up with 8 meat loaves, each about 2 inches long and 1 1/2 inches wide. Separate loaves a little bit with knife.

4 Bake uncovered for 25 minutes. To check if meat loaves are cooked, stick the meat thermometer into one loaf in the center of dish. Watch the line until it stops moving. When the line stops at 165°F, the loaves are done. If it doesn't go that high, bake loaves a little longer and test again with thermometer. Use the pot holders to take dish out of oven—it will be hot and heavy. Use the pancake turner to carefully take loaves out of dish.

1 Serving: Calories 280 (Calories from Fat 140); Total Fat 15g (Saturated Fat 6g; Trans Fat 1g); Cholesterol 125mg; Sodium 470mg; Total Carbohydrate 12g (Dietary Fiber 0g; Sugars 3g); Protein 24g   **% Daily Value:** Vitamin A 2%; Vitamin C 0%; Calcium 8%; Iron 15%   **Exchanges:** 1 Starch, 3 Medium-Fat Meat   **Carbohydrate Choices:** 1

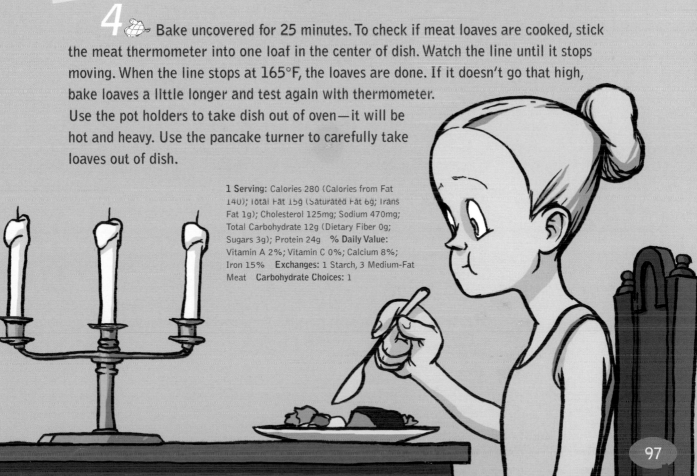

Worth-Braggin'-About Burgers

Ingredients

1 pound lean ground beef
1/4 teaspoon salt
1/8 teaspoon pepper
4 hamburger buns, split
Your favorite toppings
(ketchup, mustard, tomatoes,
lettuce, dill pickle slices)

Utensils

Ruler, if you like
Measuring spoons
Extra-large skillet
(12 inch)
Pancake turner
Meat thermometer
Sharp knife
Cookie sheet, if you like
Pot holders

Prep 15 minutes
Cook 10 minutes
Makes 4 burgers

1 Shape the **GROUND BEEF** with your hands into 4 patties. (They should be about 3/4 inch thick. Use the ruler to measure, if you like.) Sprinkle about half of the **SALT** and **PEPPER** on one side of the patties. Turn patties over, and sprinkle the rest of the salt and pepper on the other side of patties.

2 Put patties in the skillet. Cook over medium heat for 5 minutes. Flip patties over, using the pancake turner. Cook for about 5 minutes longer. To check if patties are cooked, stick the meat thermometer into one of the patties. Watch the line until it stops moving. When the line stops at 165°F, the patties are done. If it doesn't go that high, cook patties a little longer and test again with thermometer.

3 Open each **HAMBURGER BUN** to make a top and a bottom. If you like, toast the buns. Put patties on the bottoms of the buns. Add your favorite **TOPPINGS**. Cover with the tops of the buns.

✳ How to...

...**Toast Hamburger Buns:** Set the oven control to broil. Put bun halves, cut side up, on a cookie sheet. Put cookie sheet in oven so tops of buns are 4 to 5 inches from heat. Toast buns about 1 minute or until they are light brown. Watch carefully! Use the pot holders to take cookie sheet out of oven.

1 Burger: Calories 310 (Calories from Fat 130); Total Fat 15g (Saturated Fat 5g; Trans Fat 1g); Cholesterol 70mg; Sodium 410mg; Total Carbohydrate 21g (Dietary Fiber 0g; Sugars 3g); Protein 24g   % **Daily Value:** Vitamin A 0%; Vitamin C 0%; Calcium 8%; Iron 20%   **Exchanges:** 1 1/2 Starch, 3 Medium-Fat Meat   Carbohydrate Choices: 1 1/2

Sloppy Joes

Prep 15 minutes
Cook 25 minutes
Makes 12 sandwiches

Ingredients

1 large onion, if you like
2 pounds ground beef
1/4 cup water
1/2 teaspoon salt
3 tablespoons Worcestershire sauce
1/4 teaspoon red pepper sauce
1 bottle (12 ounces) chili sauce
12 hamburger buns, split

Utensils

Paper towel
Cutting board
Sharp knife
Extra-large skillet (12 inch)
Wooden spoon
Strainer
Small bowl
Liquid-ingredient measuring cup
Measuring spoons

1 If you use the **ONION**, peel off the outside layer of skin. Wash onion in cool water. Pat dry with the paper towel. Chop onion into small pieces on the cutting board, using the knife.

2 Put onion and the **GROUND BEEF** in the skillet. Stir with the wooden spoon until beef is broken into small pieces. Cook over medium heat for 8 to 10 minutes, stirring often, until beef is thoroughly cooked and browned.

3 Take skillet off hot burner. Drain beef and onion. Put beef and onion back in skillet.

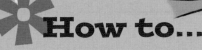
✳ How to...

...Drain Ground Beef and Onion: Put the strainer over the bowl. Spoon the beef and onion into the strainer to drain off the fat. Don't pour the fat down the kitchen drain. Put it in a container and throw it away.

4 Add the **WATER, SALT, WORCESTERSHIRE SAUCE, RED PEPPER SAUCE** and **CHILI SAUCE** to beef and onion. Cook over medium-high heat until the mixture is boiling, stirring all the time. Turn the heat down to low. Cook for 10 minutes, stirring a few times.

5 Split each **HAMBURGER BUN** in half to make a top and a bottom. Spoon about 1/2 cup of the sloppy joe mixture onto bottom of each bun. Cover with tops of buns.

1 Sandwich: Calories 280 (Calories from Fat 90);
Total Fat 10g (Saturated Fat 4g; Trans Fat 1g);
Cholesterol 45mg; Sodium 760mg; Total Carbohydrate
28g (Dietary Fiber 3g; Sugars 6g); Protein 18g
% Daily Value: Vitamin A 4%; Vitamin C 4%;
Calcium 8%; Iron 20%   **Exchanges:** 1 1/2
Starch, 1/2 Other Carbohydrate, 2 Medium-Fat
Meat   **Carbohydrate Choices:** 2

Totally Terrific Tacos

Prep 15 minutes
Cook 15 minutes
Makes 10 tacos

Ingredients

1/2 head lettuce

1 tomato

1 cup shredded Cheddar cheese (4 ounces)

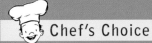 Chef's Choice

3/4 cup sour cream
or 3/4 cup guacamole
or 3/4 cup taco sauce

1 pound lean ground beef

1 cup salsa

10 taco shells

Utensils

Paper towels

Cutting board

Sharp knife

Dry-ingredient measuring cups

4 small serving bowls

Liquid-ingredient measuring cup

Extra-large skillet (12 inch)

Wooden spoon

Strainer

Small bowl

Large serving bowl

Tongs, for serving

Serving spoons, for serving

1 Wash the **LETTUCE** in cool water. Pat dry with the paper towels. Cut lettuce into long pieces on the cutting board, using the knife. Put lettuce in one of the small serving bowls.

2 Wash the **TOMATO** in cool water. Pat dry with paper towels. Chop the tomato into small pieces on cutting board, using knife. Put tomato in another small serving bowl.

3 Put the **CHEESE** in the third small serving bowl. Put the **SOUR CREAM** (or **GUACAMOLE** or **TACO SAUCE**) in the fourth small serving bowl.

4 Put the **GROUND BEEF** in the skillet. Stir with the wooden spoon until beef is broken into small pieces. Cook over medium heat 8 to 10 minutes, stirring often, until beef is thoroughly cooked and brown.

5 Take skillet off hot burner. Put the strainer over the small bowl. Spoon beef into strainer to drain the fat. Put beef back in skillet.

6 Add the **SALSA** to beef. Heat to boiling, stirring all the time. Turn the heat down to medium-low. Cook 5 minutes, stirring a few times. Pour the beef mixture into the large serving bowl.

7 Heat the **TACO SHELLS** as directed on box, if you like. Serve taco shells with beef mixture, lettuce, tomato, cheese and sour cream (or guacamole or taco sauce), letting each person make his or her own taco.

1 Taco: Calories 240 (Calories from Fat 140); Total Fat 15g (Saturated Fat 7g; Trans Fat 1.5g); Cholesterol 50mg; Sodium 260mg; Total Carbohydrate 12g (Dietary Fiber 2g; Sugars 3g); Protein 13g   **% Daily Value:** Vitamin A 10%; Vitamin C 6%; Calcium 10%; Iron 8%   **Exchanges:** 1 Starch, 1 1/2 Medium-Fat Meat, 1 1/2 Fat   **Carbohydrate Choices:** 1

Chill-Chasin' Chili

Prep 15 minutes
Cook 1 hour
Makes 4 servings

Ingredients

1 pound lean ground beef
1 can (14.5 ounces) diced tomatoes
3 teaspoons chili powder
1/2 teaspoon garlic salt

1/8 teaspoon red pepper sauce
1 can (15 to 16 ounces) red kidney beans
1/4 cup shredded Cheddar cheese (1 ounce)

Utensils

Large saucepan (3 quart)
Wooden spoon
Strainer
Small bowl
Can opener
Measuring spoons
Dry-ingredient measuring cups

1 Put the **GROUND BEEF** in the saucepan. Stir with the wooden spoon until beef is broken into small pieces. Cook over medium heat for 8 to 10 minutes, stirring often, until beef is thoroughly cooked and brown.

2 Take saucepan off hot burner. Put the strainer over the small bowl. Spoon beef into strainer to drain the fat. Put beef back in saucepan.

3 Open the can of **TOMATOES** with the can opener. Add the tomatoes (with the liquid in the can), **CHILI POWDER, GARLIC SALT** and **RED PEPPER SAUCE** to beef. Stir until mixed. Heat to boiling over medium-high heat, stirring a few times. Turn heat down to low. Cook for 30 minutes, stirring a few times.

4 Open the can of **KIDNEY BEANS** with the can opener. Add beans (with the liquid in the can) to beef mixture. Stir until mixed. Cook for 20 minutes longer.

5 Take saucepan off hot burner. Top each serving of chili with the **CHEESE**.

1 Serving: Calories 370 (Calories from Fat 140); Total Fat 16g (Saturated Fat 7g; Trans Fat 1g); Cholesterol 80mg; Sodium 590mg; Total Carbohydrate 26g (Dietary Fiber 7g; Sugars 4g); Protein 31g   % Daily Value: Vitamin A 15%; Vitamin C 10%; Calcium 10%; Iron 30%   Exchanges: 1 1/2 Starch, 4 Lean Meat, 1/2 Fat   Carbohydrate Choices: 2

Chicken Pot Pie

Prep 20 minutes
Bake 40 minutes
Cool 5 minutes
Makes 6 servings

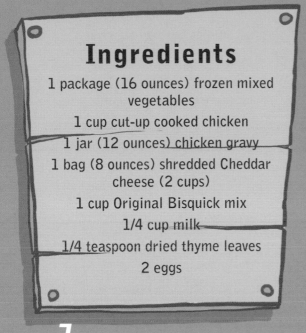

Ingredients

1 package (16 ounces) frozen mixed
vegetables

1 cup cut-up cooked chicken

1 jar (12 ounces) chicken gravy

1 bag (8 ounces) shredded Cheddar
cheese (2 cups)

1 cup Original Bisquick mix

1/4 cup milk

1/4 teaspoon dried thyme leaves

2 eggs

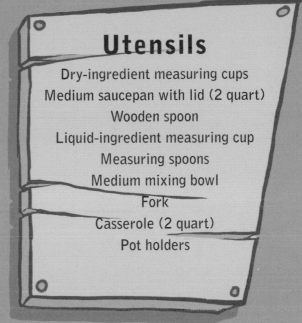

Utensils

Dry-ingredient measuring cups

Medium saucepan with lid (2 quart)

Wooden spoon

Liquid-ingredient measuring cup

Measuring spoons

Medium mixing bowl

Fork

Casserole (2 quart)

Pot holders

1 Heat the oven to 375°F. Put the **VEGETABLES**, **CHICKEN** and **GRAVY** in the saucepan. Heat over medium-high heat until boiling, stirring all the time with the wooden spoon. Take saucepan off hot burner. Cover saucepan with lid to keep the vegetable mixture warm.

2 Put the **CHEESE**, **BISQUICK MIX**, **MILK** and **THYME** in the bowl. Crack the **EGGS** on side of bowl, letting eggs slip into bowl. Stir with the fork until mixed.

3 Pour warm vegetable mixture into the casserole. Pour the cheese mixture over vegetable mixture.

4 Bake for 35 to 40 minutes or until the crust of the pot pie is golden brown. Use the pot holders to take casserole out of oven—it will be very hot and heavy. Let pot pie cool for 5 minutes.

1 Serving: Calories 420 (Calories from Fat 210); Total Fat 23g (Saturated
Fat 11g; Trans Fat 1g); Cholesterol 135mg; Sodium 930mg;
Carbohydrate 28g (Dietary Fiber 4g; Sugars 8g); Protein
24g   % Daily Value: Vitamin A 70%; Vitamin C 2%;
Calcium 35%; Iron 15%   Exchanges: 1 1/2 Starch,
1/2 Other Carbohydrate, 3 Lean Meat, 2 1/2
Fat   Carbohydrate Choices: 2

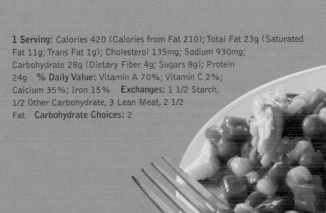

Eat 'em Up Enchiladas

Prep 15 minutes
Bake 15 minutes
Makes 5 servings

Ingredients

1 cup sour cream
1 jar (15 to 16 ounces) salsa
10 flour tortillas (8 inches across)

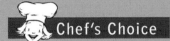 Chef's Choice

2 1/2 cups shredded cooked chicken
or 2 cans (15 ounces each) pinto beans
or 2 1/2 cups frozen cooked salad shrimp, thawed

1 cup shredded Monterey Jack cheese (4 ounces)
Extra sour cream, if you like

Utensils

Dry-ingredient measuring cups
Medium mixing bowl
Spoon
Rectangular glass baking dish
(13 × 9 inch; 3 quart)
Pot holders

1 Heat the oven to 350°F. Put the **SOUR CREAM** and **SALSA** in the bowl. Stir with the spoon until mixed.

2 Dip each **TORTILLA** into the sour cream–salsa mixture. Coat both sides of the tortilla.

3 Put 1/4 cup of the **CHICKEN** (or 1/3 cup of the **BEANS** or 1/4 cup of the **SHRIMP**) on top of each tortilla. Roll up tortilla. Put tortilla, seam-side down, in the baking dish. Pour the rest of the sour cream–salsa mixture over tortillas. Sprinkle with the **CHEESE**.

4 Bake uncovered for about 15 minutes or until cheese is melted. Use the pot holders to take dish out of oven—it will be hot and heavy. Top enchiladas with the **EXTRA SOUR CREAM**, if you like.

1 Serving: Calories 300 (Calories from Fat 120); Total Fat 14g (Saturated Fat 6g; Trans Fat 1g); Cholesterol 55mg; Sodium 490mg; Total Carbohydrate 27g (Dietary Fiber 2g; Sugars 3g); Protein 17g   % Daily Value: Vitamin A 10%; Vitamin C 6%; Calcium 20%; Iron 15%   Exchanges: 2 Starch, 1 1/2 Lean Meat, 1 1/2 Fat   Carbohydrate Choices: 2

Crunchy Chicken Tenders

Ingredients

Cooking spray
3/4 cup cornflakes cereal
1/2 cup all-purpose flour
3/4 teaspoon salt
1/2 teaspoon pepper
1/3 cup buttermilk or milk
1 pound uncooked
chicken breast tenders
(not breaded)

Utensils

Rectangular pan
(13 × 9 inch)
Foil
Dry-ingredient measuring cups
Measuring spoons
Plastic bag with zipper top
Rolling pin
Liquid-ingredient measuring cup
Medium mixing bowl
Pot holders
Sharp knife

Prep 20 minutes
Bake 30 minutes
Makes 4 servings

1 Heat the oven to 400°F. Line the pan with the foil. Spray foil with the **COOKING SPRAY**. Save for later (you will need this in step 3).

2 Put the **CEREAL**, **FLOUR**, **SALT** and **PEPPER** in the plastic bag. Seal bag closed. Use the rolling pin to crush cereal.

3 Pour the **BUTTERMILK** into the bowl. Dip the **CHICKEN** into buttermilk. Drop buttermilk-coated chicken, a few pieces at a time, into cereal mixture. Seal bag closed. Shake bag to coat chicken with cereal mixture. Put the coated chicken in the foil-lined and sprayed pan.

4 Spray chicken with cooking spray. Throw away any leftover cereal mixture in bag.

5 Bake for 25 to 30 minutes or until coating is crisp and chicken is no longer pink in center. (To check if chicken is cooked, use the pot holders to take pan out of oven, then cut into the thickest piece of chicken with the knife.)

1 Serving: Calories 190 (Calories from Fat 15); Total Fat 2g (Saturated Fat 0g; Trans Fat 0g); Cholesterol 50mg; Sodium 630mg; Total Carbohydrate 18g (Dietary Fiber 0g; Sugars 1g); Protein 27g   **% Daily Value:** Vitamin A 2%; Vitamin C 0%; Calcium 4%; Iron 15%   **Exchanges:** 1 Starch, 3 1/2 Very Lean Meat   **Carbohydrate Choices:** 1

Whatever

Prep 20 minutes
Bake 25 minutes
Cool 10 minutes
Makes 6 servings

Ingredients

Shortening (to grease pan)

1 can (13.8 ounces) refrigerated
pizza crust

1 cup pizza sauce

 Chef's Choice

1/2 cup chopped green bell pepper
or 1/2 package (3-ounce size) thinly
sliced pepperoni
or 1/4 pound cooked crumbled lean
ground beef or sausage

1 1/2 cups shredded mozzarella
cheese (6 ounces)

Utensils

Round pizza pan (12 inch)
or rectangular pan (13 × 9 inch)

Pastry brush

Pot holders

Wire cooling rack

Liquid-ingredient measuring cup

Rubber spatula

Dry-ingredient measuring cups

Pizza cutter

Pizza

1 Heat the oven to 425°F. Grease the pizza pan or rectangular pan with the **SHORTENING**, using the pastry brush.

2 Open the can of **PIZZA CRUST** and take out the dough. Unroll dough and place it in the greased pan. Starting in the center of dough, press dough to the edge of pan, using your hands.

3 Bake for about 10 minutes or until the crust is light golden brown. Use the pot holders to take pan out of oven. Cool for 5 minutes on the wire cooling rack.

4 Spread the **PIZZA SAUCE** evenly over crust, using the rubber spatula.

5 Sprinkle the **GREEN PEPPER** (or **PEPPERONI** or **GROUND BEEF** or **SAUSAGE**) over sauce. (If you like, you can use all of them.) Sprinkle the **CHEESE** over the top.

6 Use the pot holders to put pan back in oven. Bake for 12 to 15 minutes longer or until crust is golden brown and cheese is melted. Use pot holders to take pan out of oven. Cool pizza for 5 minutes. Cut into wedges, using the pizza cutter.

1 Serving: Calories 270 (Calories from Fat 80); Total Fat 8g (Saturated Fat 4.5g; Trans Fat 0.5g); Cholesterol 15mg; Sodium 800mg; Total Carbohydrate 36g (Dietary Fiber 2g; Sugars 7g); Protein 13g   **% Daily Value:** Vitamin A 6%; Vitamin C 10%; Calcium 20%; Iron 15%   **Exchanges:** 2 Starch, 1/2 Other Carbohydrate, 1 Medium-Fat Meat, 1/2 Fat   **Carbohydrate Choices:** 2 1/2

BBQ Pork Pitas

Prep 10 minutes
Cook 3 minutes
Makes 6 sandwiches

Ingredients

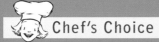 **Chef's Choice**

1 container (18 ounces) refrigerated barbecue sauce with shredded pork
or 1 container (18 ounces) refrigerated barbecue sauce with shredded chicken
or 1 container (18 ounces) refrigerated barbecue sauce with shredded beef

3 whole wheat or white pita breads (6 inches across)
3/4 cup shredded Cheddar cheese (3 ounces)

Utensils

Small saucepan (1 quart)
Wooden spoon
Cutting board
Sharp knife
Spoon
Dry-ingredient measuring cups
Measuring spoons

1 Put the **PORK** (or **CHICKEN** or **BEEF**) in the saucepan, using the wooden spoon. Cook over medium-high heat for 2 to 3 minutes or until it is bubbly and hot, stirring with wooden spoon once or twice. Take saucepan off hot burner.

2 Cut each **PITA BREAD** in half to make pockets on the cutting board, using the knife.

3 Spoon about 1/3 cup of the pork into each pita pocket. Sprinkle about 2 tablespoons of the **CHEESE** into each pocket.

1 Sandwich: Calories 260 (Calories from Fat 80); Total Fat 8g (Saturated Fat 4g; Trans Fat 0g); Cholesterol 35mg; Sodium 800mg; Total Carbohydrate 32g (Dietary Fiber 2g; Sugars 16g); Protein 15g   **% Daily Value:** Vitamin A 8%; Vitamin C 0%; Calcium 8%; Iron 10%   **Exchanges:** 1 Starch, 1 Other Carbohydrate, 1 1/2 Medium-Fat Meal   **Carbohydrate Choices:** 2

Prep 10 minutes
Cook 35 minutes
Makes 6 servings

Swirly Pasta

Ingredients

Utensils

Cutting board

Sharp knife

Paper towel

Dry-ingredient measuring cups

Measuring spoons

Large saucepan (3 quart)

2 wooden spoons

Can opener

Extra-large saucepan with lid (4 quart)

Colander

Sauce

2 cloves garlic

1 small onion

1 1/2 teaspoons olive oil

1 can (29 ounces) pureed tomatoes

1 teaspoon dried basil leaves

1 teaspoon dried oregano leaves

1/4 teaspoon salt

1/4 teaspoon pepper

Pasta

Water

16 ounces uncooked spaghetti or your favorite pasta

with Tomato Sauce

1 Peel the outside layer of skin from each of the cloves of **GARLIC**. Chop garlic cloves into tiny pieces on the cutting board, using the knife.

2 Peel the outside layer of skin from the **ONION**. Wash onion in cool water. Pat dry with the paper towel. Chop onion into small pieces on cutting board, using knife (you need about 1/4 cup.)

3 Put the **OLIVE OIL** in the large saucepan. Heat it over medium heat for about 1 minute. Put garlic and onion in oil. Cook about 3 minutes, stirring all the time with one of the wooden spoons, until onion is tender. Take saucepan off hot burner.

4 Open the can of **TOMATOES** with the can opener. Pour tomatoes into the garlic and onion mixture in saucepan. Add the **BASIL**, **OREGANO**, **SALT** and **PEPPER**. Stir with spoon until mixed. Turn the heat up to high. Heat until the mixture is boiling. Turn heat down to low. Simmer the sauce uncovered for about 30 minutes, stirring a few times.

5 While sauce is simmering, fill the very large saucepan with enough **WATER** so it is about half full. Cover saucepan with lid. Heat over medium-high heat until water is boiling fast. Add the **SPAGHETTI** to water. Heat until water boils again. Boil uncovered for 10 to 12 minutes, stirring often with the other wooden spoon, until spaghetti is soft but not mushy.

6 Pour spaghetti into the colander over the sink to drain. Serve spaghetti with sauce.

1 Serving: Calories 300 (Calories from Fat 25); Total Fat 2.5g
(Saturated Fat 0g; Trans Fat 0g); Cholesterol 0mg; Sodium 640mg;
Total Carbohydrate 58g (Dietary Fiber 6g; Sugars 8g); Protein 10g
% Daily Value: Vitamin A 15%; Vitamin C 15%; Calcium 4%;
Iron 25%   Exchanges: 3 Starch, 1/2 Other Carbohydrate,
1 Vegetable   Carbohydrate Choices: 4

Lazy-Day

Prep 20 minutes
Bake 45 minutes
Cool 15 minutes
Makes 8 servings

Ingredients

1 container (15 ounces) ricotta cheese
2 tablespoons grated Parmesan cheese
1 teaspoon Italian seasoning
1 jar (26 ounces) spaghetti sauce (3 cups)
8 uncooked lasagna noodles
1 bag (8 ounces) shredded mozzarella cheese (2 cups)

Lasagna

Utensils

Measuring spoons
Medium mixing bowl
Spoon
Liquid-ingredient measuring cup
Rectangular glass baking dish
(13 × 9 inch; 3 quart)
Pot holders
Sharp knife

1 Heat the oven to 350°F. Put the **RICOTTA CHEESE**, **PARMESAN CHEESE** and **ITALIAN SEASONING** in the bowl. Stir with the spoon until mixed.

2 Pour 1 cup of the **SPAGHETTI SAUCE** into the baking dish. With the back of spoon, spread in baking dish to cover bottom. Top with 4 of the uncooked **LASAGNA NOODLES**.

3 Spread half (1 cup) of the ricotta cheese mixture over noodles, using back of spoon. Sprinkle with half (1 cup) of the **MOZZARELLA CHEESE**.

4 Spread 1 cup of spaghetti sauce over mozzarella cheese. Make more layers with the other 4 lasagna noodles, the rest of the ricotta cheese mixture and the rest of the spaghetti sauce. (Be sure spaghetti sauce completely covers noodles.) Sprinkle with the rest of mozzarella cheese.

5 Bake for 40 to 45 minutes or until the lasagna is hot in the center and cheese is melted. Use the pot holders to take baking dish out of oven—it will be very hot and heavy. Let lasagna cool for 15 minutes. Cut into 4 rows by 2 rows, using the knife.

1 Serving: Calories 350 (Calories from Fat 130); Total Fat 14g (Saturated Fat 7g; Trans Fat 0g); Cholesterol 35mg; Sodium 700mg; Total Carbohydrate 37g (Dietary Fiber 3g; Sugars 10g); Protein 18g · % Daily Value: Vitamin A 15%; Vitamin C 8%; Calcium 40%; Iron 10% · Exchanges: 2 Starch, 1/2 Other Carbohydrate, 2 Medium-Fat Meat, 1/2 Fat · Carbohydrate Choices: 2 1/2

Speedy Spuds

Prep 15 minutes
Microwave 10 minutes
Cook 3 minutes
Makes 4 spuds

1 Spud: Calories 340 (Calories from Fat 110); Total Fat 13g (Saturated Fat 7g; Trans Fat 0g); Cholesterol 50mg; Sodium 450mg; Total Carbohydrate 40g (Dietary Fiber 5g; Sugars 5g); Protein 15g **% Daily Value:** Vitamin A 15%; Vitamin C 20%; Calcium 15%; Iron 15% **Exchanges:** 2 1/2 Starch, 1 Lean Meat, 2 Fat **Carbohydrate Choices:** 2 1/2

Ingredients

4 medium red potatoes, with peel still on
8 medium green onions
Cooking spray

Chef's Choice

3/4 cup chopped cooked ham
or 1/4 cup bacon-flavor bits or chips
or 1/4 cup chopped pepperoni

1/2 cup sour cream
1/2 cup shredded Cheddar cheese
(2 ounces)

Utensils

Vegetable brush
Fork
Microwavable plate
Pot holders
Cutting board
Sharp knife
Dry-ingredient measuring cups
Medium skillet (8 inch)
Wooden spoon
Measuring spoons
Rubber spatula

1 Scrub the **POTATOES** with the vegetable brush. Poke each potato several times with the fork (this lets the steam escape and makes it easier to split the potato open later). Put potatoes about 1 inch apart in a circle on the plate. Microwave on High for 8 to 10 minutes or until potatoes are tender. Use the pot holders to take plate out of microwave.

2 Peel the outside layer of skin from the **GREEN ONIONS**. Slice onions on the cutting board, using the knife (you need about 1/2 cup).

3 Spray the skillet with the **COOKING SPRAY**. Put the green onions and **HAM** (or **BACON BITS** or **PEPPERONI**) in skillet. Cook over medium-high heat for about 3 minutes, stirring all the time with the wooden spoon, until ham is hot. Take skillet off hot burner.

4 Cut baked potatoes lengthwise in half, using knife. (If the potatoes are too hot, hold them with a pot holder.) Fluff insides of potato with fork. Put 1 tablespoon of the **SOUR CREAM** on each potato half, using the rubber spatula to get it out of the measuring spoon. Spread sour cream a little with rubber spatula. Top each potato half evenly with some ham mixture and **CHEESE**.

Cheesy

Ingredients

1 medium stalk celery

2 cans (14 ounces each) chicken broth

1 bag (32 ounces) frozen southern-style diced hash brown potatoes, thawed

1/2 cup frozen chopped onion (from 12-ounce bag), thawed

1 cup water

1 cup milk

3 tablespoons all-purpose flour

1 bag (8 ounces) shredded Cheddar–American cheese blend (2 cups)

4 medium green onions

1/4 cup cooked real bacon pieces (from 2.8-ounce package)

Prep 15 minutes
Cook 25 minutes
Makes 6 servings

1 Wash the **CELERY** in cool water. Pat dry with the paper towel. Chop celery into small pieces on the cutting board, using the knife (you need about 1/2 cup). Open the cans of **CHICKEN BROTH** with the can opener.

2 Put celery, chicken broth, the **POTATOES**, **ONION** and **WATER** in the saucepan. Cover saucepan with lid. Cook over medium-high heat for 10 to 15 minutes.

3 Put the **MILK** in the small bowl. Add the **FLOUR**. Stir with the wire whisk until mixed. Pour milk and flour mixture into potato mixture. Turn the heat up to high. Do not cover saucepan. Cook and stir with the wooden spoon for 6 to 8 minutes or until the mixture thickens. Add the **CHEESE** to saucepan. Stir until mixed. Take saucepan off hot burner.

Potato Soup

Utensils

Paper towel

Cutting board

Sharp knife

Dry-ingredient measuring cups

Can opener

Liquid-ingredient measuring cup

Large saucepan with lid (3 quart)

Small mixing bowl

Measuring spoons

Wire whisk

Wooden spoon

6 soup bowls

Ladle

4 Peel the outside layer of skin from the **GREEN ONIONS**. Chop onions into small pieces on cutting board, using knife.

5 Spoon the soup into the bowls, using the ladle. Sprinkle the **BACON** and green onions over each serving of soup.

1 Serving: Calories 410 (Calories from Fat 140); Total Fat 15g (Saturated Fat 9g; Trans Fat 0g); Cholesterol 40mg; Sodium 1280mg; Total Carbohydrate 51g (Dietary Fiber 5g; Sugars 5g); Protein 18g % Daily Value: Vitamin A 10%; Vitamin C 15%; Calcium 30%; Iron 8% Exchanges: 3 Starch, 1/2 Other Carbohydrate, 1 1/2 High-Fat Meat Carbohydrate Choices: 3 1/2

Delicious

Desserts

Apple-

Ingredients

4 medium cooking apples
(such as Rome Beauty, Granny Smith
or Greening)

1/4 cup packed brown sugar

1/2 teaspoon ground cinnamon

1/4 cup water

1 cup all-purpose flour

2/3 cup granulated sugar

1/2 cup (1 stick) butter or margarine,
softened

Ice cream, if you like

Utensils

Cutting board

Sharp knife

Dry-ingredient measuring cups

Square pan (8 × 8 inch)

Measuring spoons

Small mixing bowl

Spoon

Liquid-ingredient measuring
cup

Medium mixing bowl

Pot holders

Wire cooling rack

Ca-Dapple Crisp

1  Heat the oven to 375°F. Cut each of the **APPLES** into 4 sections on the cutting board, using the knife. Cut out the apple core and seeds. Peel apple sections with knife.

2 Cut apple sections into slices, using the knife (you need about 4 cups). Put apple slices in the pan.

3 Put the **BROWN SUGAR** and **CINNAMON** in the small bowl. Stir with the spoon until mixed. Sprinkle sugar mixture over apples. Pour the **WATER** over apples.

4 Put the **FLOUR**, **GRANULATED SUGAR** and **BUTTER** in the medium bowl. Mix with your hands until the mixture is crumbly. Sprinkle crumbly mixture over apples.

5 Bake for 45 to 50 minutes or until apples are soft and topping is golden brown. Use the pot holders to take pan out of oven. Cool for 10 minutes on the wire cooling rack.

6 Serve with the **ICE CREAM**, if you like.

1 Serving: Calories 380 (Calories from Fat 140); Total Fat 16g (Saturated Fat 10g; Trans Fat 1g); Cholesterol 40mg; Sodium 115mg; Total Carbohydrate 58g (Dietary Fiber 2g; Sugars 40g); Protein 3g   % Daily Value: Vitamin A 10%; Vitamin C 2%; Calcium 2%; Iron 8%   Exchanges: 1 Starch, 1 Fruit, 2 Other Carbohydrate, 3 Fat   Carbohydrate Choices: 4

Chocolate-Dipped Strawberries

Ingredients

Chef's Choice

1 pint (2 cups) medium-large
strawberries (18 to 20)
or 5 bananas, each cut into 4 chunks
or 3 oranges, peeled and separated
into segments

1/2 cup semisweet chocolate chips
or white vanilla baking chips

1 teaspoon shortening
or vegetable oil

Utensils

Colander
Paper towels
Cookie sheet
Waxed paper
Dry-ingredient
measuring cups

Measuring spoons
Small saucepan
(1 quart)
Wooden spoon
Plastic wrap

1 Put the **STRAWBERRIES** in the colander. Rinse with
cool water. Gently pat strawberries dry with the paper towels
(strawberries must be completely dry for chocolate to stick). Line the cookie
sheet with the waxed paper.

2 Put the **CHOCOLATE CHIPS** and **SHORTENING** in the saucepan. Heat over low heat, stirring all
the time with the wooden spoon, until chocolate is melted.

3 Dip the lower half of each 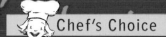 **STRAWBERRY** (or **BANANA CHUNK** or **ORANGE SEGMENT**) into
the chocolate mixture. Let the extra chocolate drip back into saucepan. Put the chocolate-
dipped fruit on paper-lined cookie sheet.

4 Put cookie sheet in the refrigerator for about 30 minutes or until chocolate is hard. Cover
any leftover chocolate-dipped fruit loosely with the plastic wrap, and put it back in the
refrigerator so the chocolate stays hard.

Chocolate Cake

Prep 30 minutes
Bake 45 minutes
Cool 1 hour 10 minutes
Makes 12 servings

Ingredients

Shortening (to grease cake pans)
2 tablespoons all-purpose flour
(to flour cake pans)
2 eggs
1 1/4 cups water
3/4 cup (1 1/2 sticks) butter
or margarine, softened

2 1/4 cups all-purpose flour
(do not use self-rising flour)
1 2/3 cups sugar
2/3 cup unsweetened baking cocoa
1 1/4 teaspoons baking soda
1 teaspoon salt
1/4 teaspoon baking powder
1 teaspoon vanilla
1 container (1 pound) your favorite flavor
ready-to-spread frosting

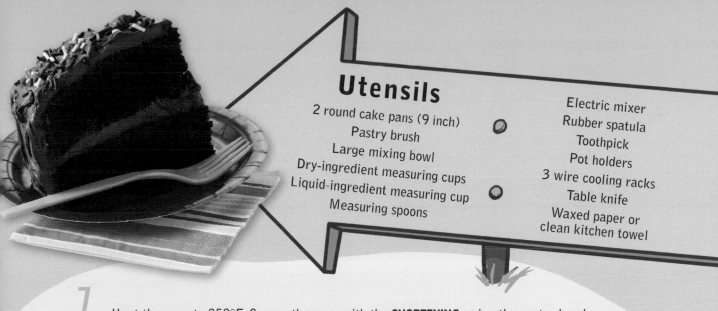

Utensils

2 round cake pans (9 inch)
Pastry brush
Large mixing bowl
Dry-ingredient measuring cups
Liquid-ingredient measuring cup
Measuring spoons

Electric mixer
Rubber spatula
Toothpick
Pot holders
3 wire cooling racks
Table knife
Waxed paper or
clean kitchen towel

1 Heat the oven to 350°F. Grease the pans with the **SHORTENING**, using the pastry brush. Sprinkle the 2 tablespoons **FLOUR** evenly over the bottom of the pans. Shake each pan back and forth to spread the flour over the bottom. Turn the pan upside down and tap the bottom so the extra flour falls out.

2 Crack the **EGGS** on side of the bowl, letting eggs slip into bowl. Add the **WATER**, **BUTTER**, 2 1/4 cups **FLOUR**, the **SUGAR**, **BAKING COCOA**, **BAKING SODA**, **SALT**, **BAKING POWDER** and **VANILLA** to egg. Beat with the electric mixer on low speed for 30 seconds. Turn off mixer. Scrape side of bowl with the rubber spatula, then beat on high speed for 3 minutes. Scrape side of bowl a few times. Pour mixture evenly into pans.

3 Bake about 30 to 35 minutes, or until the toothpick poked in center of cake comes out clean. Use the pot holders to take pans out of oven. Put each pan on a wire cooling rack. Cool cakes for 10 minutes. Take cakes out of pans. Cool cakes for about 1 hour before frosting.

How to...

...Take Cakes Out of Pans: Let each cake cool in the pan on a wire cooling rack. Run the table knife between the edge of the cake and pan. Cover the third wire cooling rack with the waxed paper or a clean kitchen towel. Put wire rack, paper side down, over pan with cake. Hold on to both wire racks with both hands, and turn upside down. Take off the pan. Put a wire cooling rack over bottom of cake. Turn upside down again. Take off top rack. Do this with both pans.

4 Put 1 cake on the serving plate. Spread about 1/3 cup of the **FROSTING** over the top of this cake, using the table knife or rubber spatula. Then stack the second cake on top of the cake on plate. Spread frosting on the side and top of the big cake.

1 Serving: Calories 500 (Calories from Fat 200); Total Fat 23g (Saturated Fat 11g; Trans Fat 0.5g); Cholesterol 65mg; Sodium 540mg; Total Carbohydrate 70g (Dietary Fiber 2g; Sugars 45g); Protein 5g   % Daily Value: Vitamin A 8%; Vitamin C 0%; Calcium 2%; Iron 15%   Exchanges: 1 1/2 Starch, 3 Other Carbohydrate, 4 1/2 Fat   Carbohydrate Choices: 4 1/2

Polka Dot

Ingredients

Cupcakes

3 eggs

1 box (1 pound 2.25 ounces)
white cake mix

1 1/4 cups water

1/3 cup vegetable oil

1 box (4-serving size)
orange-flavored
gelatin

Frosting

3 cups powdered sugar

1/3 cup butter or
margarine, softened

1 teaspoon vanilla

2 to 3 tablespoons milk

Yellow, red and blue food colors

1/3 cup white vanilla
baking chips

Utensils

24 paper baking cup
liners

Muffin pan with
12 regular-size cups

Egg separator

Small bowl (even a coffee
cup will do)

Large mixing bowl

Liquid-ingredient
measuring cup

Electric mixer

Rubber spatula

Spoon

Toothpick

Pot holders

Wire cooling racks

Dry-ingredient measuring
cups

Medium mixing bowl

4 small bowls

Table knife

Plastic wrap

132

Cupcakes

1 Heat the oven to 375°F. Put a paper baking cup liner in each muffin cup. Save for later (you will need this in step 2). Separate the **EGGS**, putting the egg whites in the large bowl. ✳

2 Add the dry **CAKE MIX**, **WATER**, **VEGETABLE OIL** and **GELATIN** to eggs. Beat with the electric mixer on low speed for 30 seconds. Beat on medium speed for 1 minute. Turn off mixer. Scrape side of bowl with the rubber spatula, then beat for 1 minute longer. Spoon the batter evenly into the paper-lined muffin cups until cups are about 2/3 full.

3 Bake for 15 to 20 minutes or until the toothpick poked in center of the cupcakes comes out clean. Use the pot holders to take muffin pans out of oven. Cool cupcakes in muffin pans for 10 minutes. Carefully tip pans on their sides to take cupcakes out of cups. Put cupcakes on the wire cooling racks. Cool cupcakes for about 30 minutes before frosting them.

4 While cupcakes are cooling, make the frosting by putting the **POWDERED SUGAR** and **BUTTER** in the medium bowl. Stir with the spoon until smooth and creamy. Add the **VANILLA** and 2 tablespoons of the **MILK**. Slowly stir, adding just enough milk to make the frosting easy to spread.

5 Divide frosting evenly among the 4 small bowls. Stir 6 drops **YELLOW FOOD COLOR** into frosting in first bowl. Stir 4 drops **RED FOOD COLOR** into frosting in second bowl. Stir 6 to 8 drops **BLUE FOOD COLOR** into frosting in third bowl. Stir 4 drops yellow and 2 drops red food color into frosting in fourth bowl.

6 Spread each color of frosting over 6 of the cupcakes, using the table knife. Poke 4 or 5 of the **VANILLA BAKING CHIPS**, flat side up, into frosting on each cupcake to look like polka dots. Cover any leftover cupcakes loosely with plastic wrap, and store at room temperature.

1 Cupcake: Calories 240 (Calories from Fat 80); Total Fat 9g (Saturated Fat 3.5g; Trans Fat 0.5g); Cholesterol 5mg; Sodium 190mg; Total Carbohydrate 37g (Dietary Fiber 0g; Sugars 29g); Protein 2g   % Daily Value: Vitamin A 0%; Vitamin C 0%; Calcium 4%; Iron 2%   Exchanges: 1/2 Starch, 2 Other Carbohydrate, 2 Fat   Carbohydrate Choices: 2 1/2

✳ How to...

...**Separate Eggs:** Put the egg separator over the small bowl. Crack 1 egg on side of bowl. Open the shell, letting yolk fall into center of egg separator. The white will slip through the slots of separator into bowl. Repeat with the rest of the eggs. Throw the yolks away.

Easy

Prep 20 minutes
Bake 52 minutes
Cool 1 hour
Refrigerate 2 hours
Makes 8 servings

Ingredients

Shortening (to grease pie plate)
3/4 cup milk
1/2 teaspoon almond extract
1 cup sugar
2 tablespoons all-purpose flour
1/2 teaspoon salt
2 eggs
2 packages (8 ounces each) cream cheese, softened
3 to 4 tablespoons your favorite ice-cream topping
About 1 cup fresh berries, if you like

Utensils

Glass pie plate (9 inch)
Pastry brush
Liquid-ingredient measuring cup
Measuring spoons
Dry-ingredient measuring cups
Blender with lid
Cutting board
Table knife
Pot holders
Wire cooling rack
Sharp knife
8 dessert plates
Plastic wrap

1 Heat the oven to 325°F. Grease the pie plate with the **SHORTENING**, using the pastry brush. Save pie plate for later (you will need it in step 3).

2 Put the **MILK**, **ALMOND EXTRACT**, **SUGAR**, **FLOUR** and **SALT** in the blender. Crack the **EGGS** on side of blender, letting eggs slip into blender. Cover blender with lid. Blend on high speed for about 15 seconds.

3 Cut the **CREAM CHEESE** into little cubes on the cutting board, using the table knife. Add cream cheese to blender. Cover blender with lid. Blend 1 minute. Pour the mixture into the greased pie plate.

Cheesecake

4  Bake for 48 to 52 minutes or until the cheesecake is slightly jiggly when pie plate is shaken. Use the pot holders to take pie plate out of oven, and place it on the wire cooling rack. Let cheesecake cool for 1 hour. Put cheesecake in the refrigerator for at least 2 hours but no longer than 48 hours.

5 Cut cheesecake into 8 slices, using the sharp knife. Put the slices on the dessert plates. Drizzle the **ICE CREAM TOPPING** over slices of cheesecake. If you like, sprinkle the berries over top of cheesecake slices. Serve right away. Cover any leftover cheesecake with the plastic wrap, and put it in the refrigerator.

1 Serving: Calories 360 (Calories from Fat 200); Total Fat 22g (Saturated Fat 13g; Trans Fat 0.5g); Cholesterol 115mg; Sodium 370mg; Total Carbohydrate 34g (Dietary Fiber 0g; Sugars 31g); Protein 7g **% Daily Value:** Vitamin A 20%; Vitamin C 0%; Calcium 8%; Iron 6% **Exchanges:** 2 Other Carbohydrate, 1 High-Fat Meat, 3 Fat **Carbohydrate Choices:** 2

Chocolate-Overload Brownies

Prep 30 minutes
Bake 45 minutes
Cool 1 hour
Makes 24 brownies

Ingredients

Brownies
Shortening (to grease pan)
5 ounces unsweetened baking chocolate
2/3 cup butter or margarine

3 eggs
1 3/4 cups granulated sugar
2 teaspoons vanilla
1 cup all-purpose flour
1 bag (6 ounces) semisweet chocolate chips (1 cup)
1 cup chopped nuts, if you like

Chocolate Frosting
2 ounces unsweetened baking chocolate
2 tablespoons butter or margarine
2 cups powdered sugar
3 tablespoons hot water

Utensils

Square pan (9 × 9 inch)
Pastry brush
2 medium saucepans (2 quart)
2 wooden spoons
Large mixing bowl

Dry-ingredient measuring cups
Measuring spoons
Electric mixer
Pot holders
Wire cooling rack
Table knife or small metal spatula

1 Heat the oven to 350°F. Grease the pan with the **SHORTENING**, using the pastry brush. Save for later (you will need this in step 5).

2 Put the 5 ounces **CHOCOLATE** and 2/3 cup **BUTTER** in one of the saucepans. Heat over low heat, stirring a few times with one of the wooden spoons, until chocolate is melted. Take saucepan off hot burner. Cool for 5 minutes.

3 Crack the **EGGS** on side of the bowl, letting eggs slip into bowl. Add the **GRANULATED SUGAR** and **VANILLA** to eggs. Beat with the electric mixer on high speed for 5 minutes.

4 Add the melted chocolate mixture to sugar mixture. Beat with electric mixer on low speed for 2 minutes. Add the **FLOUR** to chocolate mixture. Stir with wooden spoon until mixed.

5 Stir in the **CHOCOLATE CHIPS** and, if you like, the **NUTS**. Spread the batter in the greased pan, using the back of the spoon.

6 Bake for 40 to 45 minutes or just until the brownies begin to pull away from sides of pan. Use the pot holders to take pan out of oven. Put pan on the wire cooling rack. Cool brownies for 1 hour before frosting them.

7 To make the Chocolate Frosting, put the 2 ounces **CHOCOLATE** and 2 tablespoons **BUTTER** in the second saucepan. Heat over low heat, stirring a few times with the second wooden spoon, until chocolate is melted. Take saucepan off hot burner.

8 Add the **POWDERED SUGAR** and **HOT WATER** to chocolate mixture. Stir until smooth.

9 Spread frosting over brownies, using the table knife or metal spatula. Cut pan of brownies into 6 rows by 4 rows, using table knife.

1 Brownie: Calories 270 (Calories from Fat 120); Total Fat 13g (Saturated Fat 8g; Trans Fat 0.5g); Cholesterol 40mg; Sodium 60mg; Total Carbohydrate 36g (Dietary Fiber 2g; Sugars 28g); Protein 3g   % **Daily Value:** Vitamin A 4%; Vitamin C 0%; Calcium 0%; Iron 10%   **Exchanges:** 1 Starch, 1 1/2 Other Carbohydrate, 2 1/2 Fat   **Carbohydrate Choices:** 2 1/2

Chocolate Chip Cookies

Ingredients

1 egg
1/2 cup granulated sugar
1/2 cup packed brown sugar
1/2 cup (1 stick) butter or margarine, softened
1 1/2 cups all-purpose flour
1/2 teaspoon baking soda
1/2 teaspoon salt

 Chef's Choice

1 cup semisweet chocolate chips
or 1 cup candy-coated
chocolate candies
or 1 cup toffee bits

Utensils

Large mixing bowl
Dry-ingredient measuring cups
Wooden spoon
Measuring spoons
2 cookie sheets
Pot holders
Pancake turner
Wire cooling racks

1 Heat the oven to 375°F. Crack the **EGG** on side of the bowl, letting egg slip into bowl. Add the **GRANULATED SUGAR**, **BROWN SUGAR** and **BUTTER** to egg. Stir with the wooden spoon until mixed.

2 Add the **FLOUR**, **BAKING SODA** and **SALT** to sugar mixture. Stir with spoon until mixed.

3 Stir the **CHOCOLATE CHIPS** (or **CANDY-COATED CHOCOLATE CANDIES** or **TOFFEE BITS**) into the dough. Drop 12 rounded tablespoonfuls of dough onto one of the cookie sheets (you do not need to grease the cookie sheets).

4 Bake for 10 to 12 minutes or until cookies are light brown. You will need to do this 1 more time to use up all the dough.

5 Use the pot holders to take cookie sheets out of oven. Cool cookies on cookie sheets for 1 minute. Take cookies off cookie sheets, using the pancake turner, and put them on the wire cooling racks to finish cooling.

1 Cookie: Calories 140 (Calories from Fat 60), Total Fat 6g (Saturated Fat 4g; Trans Fat 0g); Cholesterol 20mg; Sodium 110mg; Total Carbohydrate 19g (Dietary Fiber 0g; Sugars 12g); Protein 1g   % Daily Value: Vitamin A 2%; Vitamin C 0%; Calcium 0%; Iron 4%   Exchanges: 1/2 Starch, 1 Other Carbohydrate, 1 Fat   Carbohydrate Choices: 1

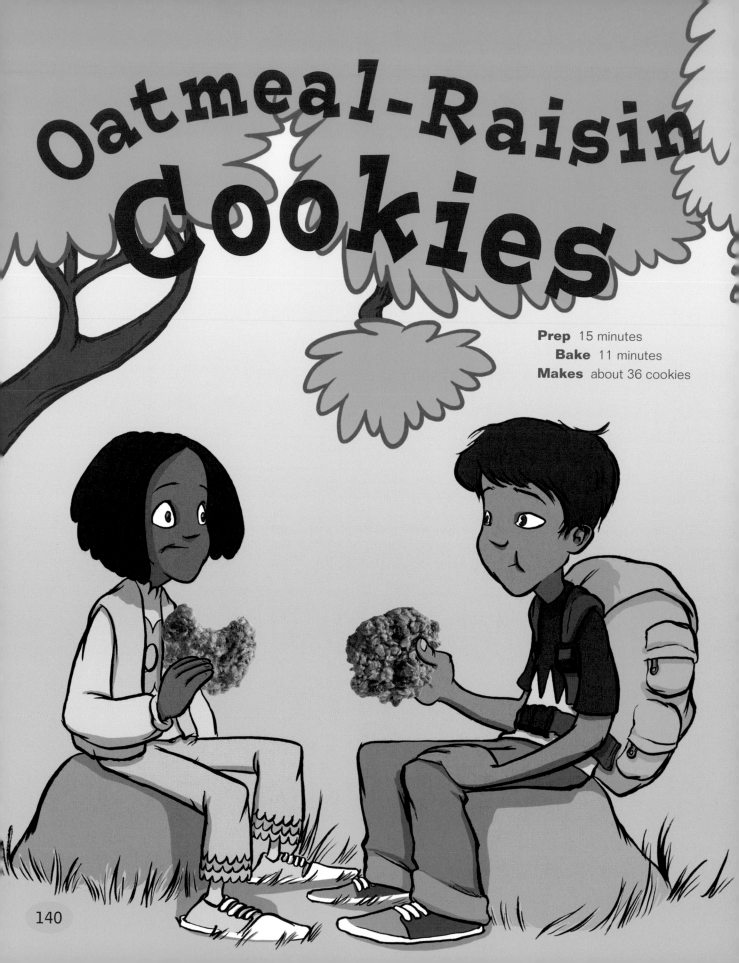

Oatmeal-Raisin Cookies

Prep 15 minutes
Bake 11 minutes
Makes about 36 cookies

Ingredients

2 eggs
2/3 cup granulated sugar
2/3 cup packed brown sugar
1/2 cup (1 stick) butter or margarine, softened
1/2 cup shortening
1 teaspoon baking soda
1 teaspoon ground cinnamon
1 teaspoon vanilla
1/2 teaspoon baking powder
1/2 teaspoon salt
3 cups quick-cooking or old-fashioned oats
1 cup all-purpose flour
1 cup raisins

Utensils

Large mixing bowl
Dry-ingredient measuring cups
Measuring spoons
Wooden spoon
3 cookie sheets
Pot holders
Pancake turner
Wire cooling racks

1 Heat the oven to 375°F. Crack the **EGGS** on side of the bowl, letting eggs slip into bowl. Add the **GRANULATED SUGAR**, **BROWN SUGAR**, **BUTTER**, **SHORTENING**, **BAKING SODA**, **CINNAMON**, **VANILLA**, **BAKING POWDER** and **SALT** to eggs. Stir with the wooden spoon until mixed.

2 Add the **OATS**, **FLOUR** and **RAISINS** to sugar mixture. Stir with spoon until mixed.

3 Drop 12 rounded tablespoonfuls of dough onto one of the cookie sheets (you do not need to grease the cookie sheets).

4 Bake for 9 to 11 minutes or until cookies are light brown. You will need to do this 2 more times to use up all the dough.

5 Use the pot holders to take cookie sheets out of oven. Take cookies off cookie sheets, using the pancake turner, and put them on the wire cooling racks to finish cooling.

1 Cookie: Calories 140 (Calories from Fat 60); Total Fat 6g (Saturated Fat 2.5g; Trans Fat 0.5g); Cholesterol 20mg; Sodium 100mg; Total Carbohydrate 18g (Dietary Fiber 1g; Sugars 10g); Protein 2g   % Daily Value: Vitamin A 0%; Vitamin C 0%; Calcium 0%; Iron 4%   Exchanges: 1/2 Starch, 1/2 Other Carbohydrate, 1 1/2 Fat   Carbohydrate Choices: 1

Topsy-Turvy Cookie Pizza

Prep 30 minutes
Bake 15 minutes
Cool 10 minutes
Cook 5 minutes
Makes 16 servings

Ingredients

Crust

Shortening (to grease pizza pan)
1 egg
1/2 cup packed brown sugar
1/4 cup granulated sugar
1/2 cup (1 stick) butter or margarine, softened
1 teaspoon vanilla
1 1/4 cups all-purpose flour
1/2 teaspoon baking soda

Chocolate Sauce

1 cup semisweet chocolate chips
2 tablespoons butter or margarine
3 tablespoons milk
1 cup powdered sugar
1/2 cup candy-coated chocolate candies

Utensils

Round pizza pan (12 inch)
Pastry brush
Medium mixing bowl
Dry-ingredient measuring cups
Measuring spoons
Wooden spoon
Pot holders
Wire cooling rack
Small saucepan (1 quart)
Small metal spatula
Pizza cutter or sharp knife

1 Heat the oven to 350°F. Grease the pizza pan with the **SHORTENING**, using the pastry brush. Save for later (you will need this in step 4).

2 Crack the **EGG** on side of the bowl, letting egg slip into bowl. Add the **BROWN SUGAR**, **GRANULATED SUGAR**, 1/2 cup **BUTTER** and the **VANILLA** to egg. Stir with the wooden spoon until mixed.

3 Add the **FLOUR** and **BAKING SODA** to sugar mixture. Stir until mixed (the dough will be stiff).

4 Spread or pat dough in the greased pizza pan to the edge, using the back of the spoon or your hands.

5 Bake for about 15 minutes or until crust is golden brown. Use the pot holders to take pan out of oven. Put pan on the wire cooling rack. Cool crust for about 10 minutes before spreading with sauce.

6 While crust is cooling, make the Chocolate Sauce by putting the **CHOCOLATE CHIPS**, 2 tablespoons **BUTTER** and **MILK** in the saucepan. Cook over low heat about 5 minutes, stirring all the time with the wooden spoon, just until chocolate chips are melted. Take saucepan off hot burner.

7 Add the **POWDERED SUGAR** to chocolate mixture. Stir until smooth and shiny. Spread sauce over cooled crust, using the metal spatula.

8 Right away, sprinkle with the **CANDIES**. Cut the pizza into 16 slices, using the pizza cutter or knife.

1 Serving: Calories 270 (Calories from Fat 110); Total Fat 12g (Saturated Fat 7g; Trans Fat 0g); Cholesterol 35mg; Sodium 105mg; Total Carbohydrate 36g (Dietary Fiber 1g; Sugars 27g); Protein 2g   % Daily Value: Vitamin A 6%; Vitamin C 0%; Calcium 2%; Iron 6%   Exchanges: 1/2 Starch, 2 Other Carbohydrate, 2 1/2 Fat   Carbohydrate Choices: 2 1/2

Peanut Butter-Ice Cream Sandwiches

Ingredients

1/4 cup sugar

1 egg

 Chef's Choice

1 pouch (1 pound 1.5 ounces) peanut butter cookie mix

or 1 pouch (1 pound 1.5 ounces) chocolate chip cookie mix

or 1 pouch (1 pound 1.5 ounces) oatmeal chocolate chip cookie mix

1/3 cup vegetable oil

4 1/2 cups vanilla ice cream

Chopped peanuts or tiny candies, if you like

Utensils

Dry-ingredient measuring cups

Small bowl

Medium mixing bowl

Liquid-ingredient measuring cup

Wooden spoon

Ruler, if you like

3 cookie sheets

Fork

Pot holders

Pancake turner

Wire cooling racks

Rectangular pan with sides (15 × 10 inch)

Plastic wrap

Prep 25 minutes
Bake 9 minutes
Cool 32 minutes
Stand 10 minutes
Freeze 30 minutes
Makes 18 ice cream sandwiches

1   Heat the oven to 375°F. Put the **SUGAR** in the small bowl. Save it for later (you will need it in step 3).

2   Crack the **EGG** on side of the medium bowl, letting egg slip into bowl. Add the **PEANUT BUTTER COOKIE MIX** (or **CHOCOLATE CHIP** or **OATMEAL CHOCOLATE CHIP**) and **VEGETABLE OIL** to egg. Stir with the wooden spoon until you get a soft dough.

3   Shape some of the dough into 12 balls, each about 1 inch across. (The balls should be about the size of a quarter. Use the ruler to measure, if you like.) Put balls about 2 inches apart on 1 of the cookie sheets (you do not need to grease the cookie sheets). Dip the fork into sugar in small bowl and firmly press fork in a crisscross pattern on each ball.

4   Bake for 7 to 9 minutes or until the edges of cookie are light brown. You will need to do this 2 more times to use up all the dough.

5   Use the pot holders to take cookie sheets out of oven. Cool cookies on cookie sheets for 2 minutes. Take cookies off cookie sheets, using the pancake turner, and put them on the wire cooling racks to finish cooling. Let cookies cool completely, about 30 minutes.

6   Take the container of ice cream out of the freezer. Put it on the counter for about 10 minutes or until the ice cream is a little soft.

7   For each ice cream sandwich, scoop about 1/4 cup softened **ICE CREAM** and put it between 2 cookies. Roll the ice cream edges in the **CHOPPED PEANUTS** or **TINY CANDIES,** or both, if you like. Put the sandwiches on the pan. Put pan in the freezer and freeze about 30 minutes or until ice cream is hard. Wrap any leftover sandwiches with the plastic wrap, and put them back in the freezer.

1 Ice Cream Sandwich: Calories 250 (Calories from Fat 110); Total Fat 12g (Saturated Fat 4g; Trans Fat 0g); Cholesterol 30mg; Sodium 170mg; Total Carbohydrate 31g (Dietary Fiber 0g; Sugars 21g); Protein 4g   % Daily Value: Vitamin A 4%; Vitamin C 0%; Calcium 4%; Iron 2%   Exchanges: 1 Starch, 1 Other Carbohydrate, 2 1/2 Fat   Carbohydrate Choices: 2

Frozen Yogurt Crunch Cups

Prep 20 minutes
Freeze 3 hours
Makes 12 servings

Ingredients

4 pouches (1.5 ounces each)
peanut butter crunchy granola bars
(from 8.9-ounce box)
1/4 cup chocolate-flavored syrup
4 cups vanilla fat-free frozen yogurt

Utensils

12 paper baking cup liners
Muffin pan with 12 regular-size cups
Rolling pin
Liquid-ingredient measuring cup
Measuring spoons
Spoon
Dry-ingredient measuring cups
Plastic wrap

1 Put a paper baking cup liner in each muffin cup. Use the rolling pin to crush the **GRANOLA BARS** in their pouches. Carefully open 2 of the pouches, and sprinkle about 1 tablespoon granola crumbs into the bottom of each muffin cup.

2 Drizzle about 1/2 teaspoon of the **CHOCOLATE SYRUP** over granola crumbs in each muffin cup, using up about half the chocolate syrup. Spoon 1/3 cup of the **FROZEN YOGURT** on top of drizzled chocolate and crumbs in each cup. Smooth yogurt, using the back of the spoon. Drizzle the rest of the chocolate syrup over yogurt in each cup (about 1/2 teaspoon on each).

3 Carefully open the other 2 pouches of granola bars. Sprinkle about 1 tablespoon crumbs over chocolate syrup in each cup. Press crumbs gently into top, using your fingers.

4 Put the muffin pan in the freezer. Freeze the cups for about 3 hours or until hard. Peel back the paper to eat. Wrap any leftover yogurt crunch cups tightly with the plastic wrap, and put them in the freezer.

1 Serving: Calories 150 (Calories from Fat 20); Total Fat 2g (Saturated Fat 0g; Trans Fat 0g); Cholesterol 0mg; Sodium 100mg; Total Carbohydrate 28g (Dietary Fiber 2g; Sugars 20g); Protein 5g **% Daily Value:** Vitamin A 0%; Vitamin C 0%; Calcium 15%; Iron 2% **Exchanges:** 1 1/2 Other Carbohydrate, 1/2 Skim Milk **Carbohydrate Choices:** 2

Indoor

Prep 20 minutes
Refrigerate 1 hour
Makes 48 bars

Ingredients

Cooking spray

12 graham cracker squares

3 cups milk chocolate chips

2 tablespoons peanut butter

3 cups miniature marshmallows

Utensils

Rectangular pan (13 × 9 inch)

Plastic bag with zipper top

Dry-ingredient measuring cups

Measuring spoons

Large saucepan (3 quart)

Wooden spoon

Sharp knife

Plastic wrap

S'mores

1 Spray the pan with the **COOKING SPRAY**. Save for later (you will need this in step 4).

2 Put the **GRAHAM CRACKERS** in the plastic bag. Seal bag closed. Squeeze the bag until crackers are broken into small pieces. (The pieces should be about the size of a postage stamp.)

3 Put the **CHOCOLATE CHIPS** and **PEANUT BUTTER** in the saucepan. Cook over low heat, stirring all the time with the wooden spoon, until chocolate chips are melted. Take saucepan off hot burner. Stir in the graham cracker pieces and **MARSHMALLOWS**.

4 Spread the marshmallow mixture in the sprayed pan, using back of wooden spoon. Put pan of bars in the refrigerator for about 1 hour or until firm. Cut the pan of bars into 8 rows by 6 rows, using the knife. Wrap any leftover bars with plastic wrap, and put them back in the refrigerator.

1 Bar: Calories 80 (Calories from Fat 35); Total Fat 3.5g (Saturated Fat 1.5g; Trans Fat 0g); Cholesterol 0mg; Sodium 25mg; Total Carbohydrate 10g (Dietary Fiber 0g; Sugars 8g); Protein 1g   % Daily Value: Vitamin A 0%; Vitamin C 0%; Calcium 2%; Iron 0%   Exchanges: 1/2 Other Carbohydrate, 1 Fat   Carbohydrate Choices: 1/2

Fabulous Fudge

Prep 20 minutes
Refrigerate 1 hour 30 minutes
Makes about 32 pieces

FUDGE O'MATIC

1 Piece: Calories 130 (Calories from Fat 50); Total Fat 6g (Saturated Fat 3.5g; Trans Fat 0g); Cholesterol 0mg; Sodium 25mg; Total Carbohydrate 17g (Dietary Fiber 0g; Sugars 15g); Protein 2g **% Daily Value:** Vitamin A 0%; Vitamin C 0%; Calcium 4%; Iron 2% **Exchanges:** 1 Other Carbohydrate, 1 1/2 Fat **Carbohydrate Choices:** 1

Ingredients

Cooking spray

3 cups semisweet chocolate chips

1 can (14 ounces) sweetened condensed milk

1/8 teaspoon salt

1 teaspoon vanilla

Decorating icing (any color), if you like

Utensils

Foil

Square pan (8 × 8 inch)

Dry-ingredient measuring cups

Medium saucepan (2 quart)

Wooden spoon

Can opener

Measuring spoons

Rubber spatula

Cutting board

Sharp knife

Airtight container

1 Tear off a sheet of foil that is 14 inches long. Gently press the foil into the pan so that it covers the bottom and goes up the sides. Spray the foil on bottom and sides with the **COOKING SPRAY.** Save pan for later (you will need it in step 4).

2 Put the **CHOCOLATE CHIPS** in the saucepan. Cook over low heat, stirring a few times with the wooden spoon, until chocolate chips are melted. Take saucepan off hot burner.

3 Open the can of **SWEETENED CONDENSED MILK**, using the can opener. Add the sweetened condensed milk, **SALT** and **VANILLA** to the melted chocolate. Stir with spoon until mixed.

4 Pour the chocolate mixture into sprayed, foil-lined pan. Spread mixture evenly with the rubber spatula. Put pan in the refrigerator for about 1 hour 30 minutes or until the fudge is firm.

5 Hold on to foil on 2 sides of pan with both hands. Lift foil and fudge out of pan. Turn fudge upside down on the cutting board, and peel off foil. Cut fudge into 8 rows by 4 rows, using the knife. Decorate fudge with the **DECORATING ICING**, if you like. Put any leftover fudge the airtight container, and put it in the refrigerator.

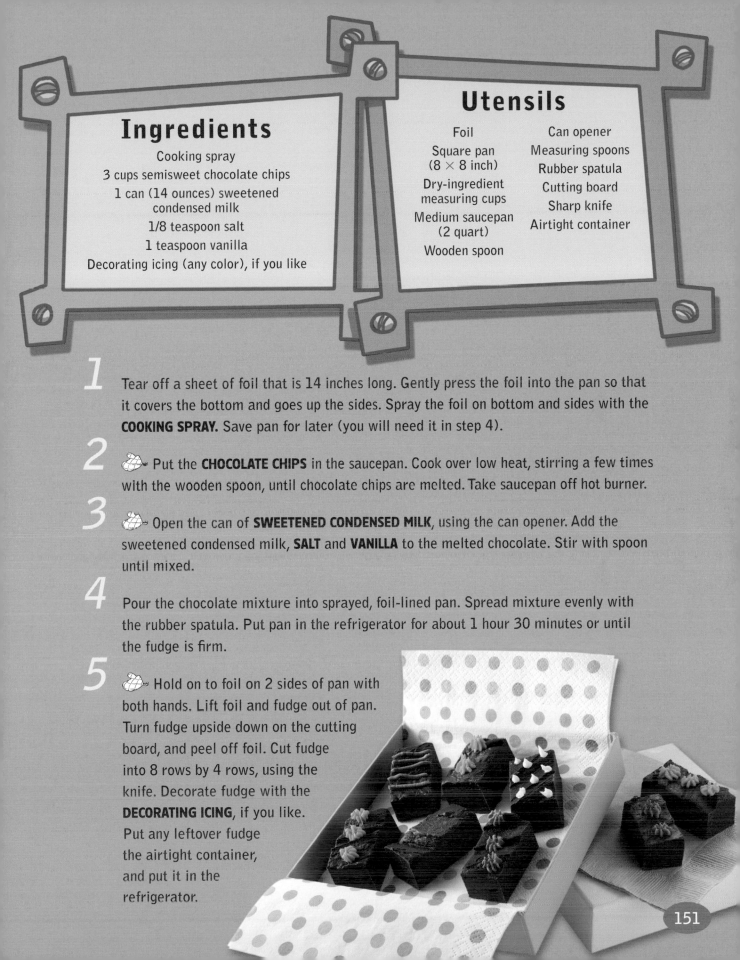

Make It! Shake It!

Ingredients

3/4 cup milk

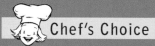 Chef's Choice

1/4 cup chocolate-flavored syrup
or 1/4 cup caramel topping
or 1/4 cup butterscotch topping

3 large scoops vanilla ice cream
(about 1 1/2 cups total)

Utensils

Liquid-ingredient
measuring cup

Ice cream scoop

Blender with lid

2 tall drinking glasses

2 drinking straws

Prep 10 minutes
Makes 2 servings

1 Serving: Calories 380 (Calories from Fat 130); Total Fat
14g (Saturated Fat 9g; Trans Fat 0.5g); Cholesterol 55mg;
Sodium 150mg; Total Carbohydrate 55g (Dietary Fiber 2g;
Sugars 42g); Protein 8g   % Daily Value: Vitamin A 15%;
Vitamin C 0%; Calcium 25%; Iron 6%   Exchanges: 3 Other
Carbohydrate, 1 Low-Fat Milk, 2 Fat   Carbohydrate Choices:
3 1/2

Milk Shakes

1 Put the **MILK**,  **CHOCOLATE SYRUP** (or **CARAMEL TOPPING** or **BUTTERSCOTCH TOPPING**) and **ICE CREAM** in the blender. Cover blender with lid, and blend on low speed about 10 seconds or until smooth.

2 Pour the shake into the drinking glasses. Put a straw in each glass, and serve right away.

Helpful Nutrition and Cooking Information

Nutrition Guidelines

We provide nutrition information for each recipe that includes calories, fat, cholesterol, sodium, carbohydrate, fiber, sugar and protein. Also included are % of Daily Value, Exchanges and Carbohydrate Choices. Individual food choices can be based on this information.

Recommended intake for a daily diet of 2,000 calories as set by the Food and Drug Administration

Total Fat	Less than 65g
Saturated Fat	Less than 20g
Cholesterol	Less than 300mg
Sodium	Less than 2,400mg
Total Carbohydrate	300g
Dietary Fiber	25g

Criteria Used for Calculating Nutrition Information

- The first ingredient was used wherever a choice is given (such as 1/3 cup sour cream or plain yogurt).

- The first ingredient amount was used wherever a range is given (such as 3- to 3-1/2–pound cut-up broiler-fryer chicken).

- The first serving number was used wherever a range is given (such as 4 to 6 servings).

- "If desired" ingredients and recipe variations were not included (such as sprinkle with brown sugar, if desired).

Ingredients Used in Recipe Testing and Nutrition Calculations

- Ingredients used for testing represent those that the majority of consumers use in their homes: large eggs, 2% milk, 80%-lean ground beef, canned ready-to-use chicken broth.

- Fat-free, low-fat or low-sodium products were not used, unless otherwise indicated.

- Solid vegetable shortening (not butter, margarine or cooking sprays) was used to grease pans, unless otherwise indicated.

Equipment Used in Recipe Testing

We use equipment for testing that the majority of consumers use in their homes. If a specific piece of equipment is necessary for recipe success, it is listed in the recipe.

- Cookware and bakeware without nonstick coatings were used, unless otherwise indicated.

- No dark-colored, black or insulated bakeware was used.

- When a pan is specified in a recipe, a metal pan was used; a baking dish or pie plate means ovenproof glass was used.

- An electric hand mixer was used for mixing only when mixer speeds are specified in the recipe directions. When a mixer speed is not given, a spoon or fork was used.

Metric Conversion Guide

VOLUME

U.S. Units	Canadian Metric	Australian Metric
1/4 teaspoon	1 mL	1 ml
1/2 teaspoon	2 mL	2 ml
1 teaspoon	5 mL	5 ml
1 tablespoon	15 mL	20 ml
1/4 cup	50 mL	60 ml
1/3 cup	75 mL	80 ml
1/2 cup	125 mL	125 ml
2/3 cup	150 mL	170 ml
3/4 cup	175 mL	190 ml
1 cup	250 mL	250 ml
1 quart	1 liter	1 liter
1 1/2 quarts	1.5 liters	1.5 liters
2 quarts	2 liters	2 liters
2 1/2 quarts	2.5 liters	2.5 liters
3 quarts	3 liters	3 liters
4 quarts	4 liters	4 liters

WEIGHT

U.S. Units	Canadian Metric	Australian Metric
1 ounce	30 grams	30 grams
2 ounces	55 grams	60 grams
3 ounces	85 grams	90 grams
4 ounces (1/4 pound)	115 grams	125 grams
8 ounces (1/2 pound)	225 grams	225 grams
16 ounces (1 pound)	455 grams	500 grams
1 pound	455 grams	1/2 kilogram

MEASUREMENTS

Inches	Centimeters
1	2.5
2	5.0
3	7.5
4	10.0
5	12.5
6	15.0
7	17.5
8	20.5
9	23.0
10	25.5
11	28.0
12	30.5
13	33.0

TEMPERATURES

Fahrenheit	Celsius
32°	0°
212°	100°
250°	120°
275°	140°
300°	150°
325°	160°
350°	180°
375°	190°
400°	200°
425°	220°
450°	230°
475°	240°
500°	260°

NOTE: The recipes in this cookbook have not been developed or tested using metric measures. When converting recipes to metric, some variations in quality may be noted.

Index

T

W

Y

Complete your cookbook library
with these *Betty Crocker* titles

Betty Crocker's Christmas Cookbook

Betty Crocker's Bisquick® Cookbook

Betty Crocker Bisquick® II Cookbook

Betty Crocker Bisquick® Impossibly Easy Pies

Betty Crocker Celebrate!

Betty Crocker's Cook Book for Boys and Girls

Betty Crocker Cookbook, 10th Edition— *The* **BIG RED** *Cookbook*®

Betty Crocker Cookbook, Bridal Edition

Betty Crocker Cookbook for Women

Betty Crocker's Cookie Book

Betty Crocker's Cooking Basics

Betty Crocker's Cooky Book, Facsimile Edition

Betty Crocker Decorating Cakes and Cupcakes

Betty Crocker's Diabetes Cookbook

Betty Crocker Easy Everyday Vegetarian

Betty Crocker Easy Family Dinners

Betty Crocker's Entertaining Basics

Betty Crocker 4-Ingredient Dinners

Betty Crocker Grilling Made Easy

Betty Crocker Healthy Heart Cookbook

Betty Crocker's Indian Home Cooking

Betty Crocker's Italian Cooking

Betty Crocker Just the Two of Us

Betty Crocker's Kitchen Library

Betty Crocker's Living with Cancer Cookbook

Betty Crocker's Low-Fat, Low-Cholesterol Cooking Today

Betty Crocker More Slow Cooker Recipes

Betty Crocker One-Dish Meals

Betty Crocker's A Passion for Pasta

Betty Crocker's Picture Cook Book, Facsimile Edition

Betty Crocker Quick & Easy Cookbook

Betty Crocker's Slow Cooker Cookbook

Betty Crocker's Ultimate Cake Mix Cookbook

Betty Crocker Why It Works

Betty Crocker Win at Weight Loss Cookbook

Cocina Betty Crocker